WARMAN'S

Antique
American Games

1840—1940

LEE DENNIS

Wallace-Homestead Book Company
Radnor, Pennsylvania

Published in Radnor, Pennsylvania 19089, by Wallace-Homestead,
a division of Chilton Book Company

ISBN: 0-87069-630-0 (pbk)
ISBN: 0-87069-631-9 (hardcover)
ISSN: 0882-5386
Library of Congress Catalog Card No.:   85-050969

Manufactured in the United States of America

1 2 3 4 5 6 7 8 9 0   0 9 8 7 6 5 4 3 2 1

CONTENTS

COLLECTING ANTIQUE GAMES IN THE 1990s

A dozen or so years ago, you could readily find good vintage games on the open market. All this has changed. Now, the most desirable games are in excellent private collections, and thankfully are being preserved as colorful boxes of Americana. Sadly, much of what remains on the market are the most common games in various degrees of deterioration.

To find games of value in good condition today, try to buy them from a private collection, at the auction and/or room selling at the American Game Collectors Association (AGCA) annual convention, or bid games at an auction sale of a well-cared-for toy or game collection.

Prices of small card games have risen little or not at all, with the exception of early ones from the 1840s and 1850s. Several, notably *Authors, Pit, Rook* and *Flinch,* have decreased in value. Religious, educational, and Bingo-type games and cheaply made compendiums of games are also in low demand.

Playability still has little to do with the desirability of an antique game; condition, subject matter, graphics, and rarity have *everything* to do with value. Fortunately, little in the games field has been reproduced, so the earliest hand-painted American board games are now regarded as artistic forms, particularly when enhanced by conservation technique framing.

Almost all McLoughlin games have appreciated—many several times beyond their original cost. Once fairly obtainable, the large McLoughlin game is now an endangered species. Oversized Parker Brothers games are following suit, albeit at a slower pace. Any games connected with golf, baseball, Oz, blacks, railroading, and other "hot" subjects will continue to rise in price and scarcity.

Through the research efforts of dedicated members of the AGCA, more and more information is coming to light regarding the history of lesser-known game companies. In 1986, the AGCA established excellent archives of game-related material, such as extra copies of rules, catalogs, advertising, and other game memorabilia. The club now mails to members two outstanding publications, *Game Times* (three times a year) and *Game Researchers Notes (GRN)*, which are invaluable to any collector of antique games.

An increasing number of collectors has intensified the hunt for this country's early games. Diligence and discrimination will determine the rewards of this search.

Lee Dennis
May, 1991

INTRODUCTION

Once regarded as mere adjuncts to the toy field, games now are finding a collector's niche for themselves. Much has been written on dolls, toys, trains, banks, and other related categories, but little information exists solely on American board and card games.

The brilliant lithography on the box covers and boards of games lures more collectors each year. The colorful graphics of antique games always have accurately portrayed the ongoing saga of this country's mores and history. Through the imaginative drawings of commercial, yet largely unknown, artists, admirers of old boxed games can view the transportation of yesterday by trolley or transoceanic steamship, recall the discoveries of Pike's Peak or the North Pole, note the helmetless uniforms of an 1895 football team or the leg puttees of a vintage motorcyclist, trace the mapped strategies of long past battles and naval engagements, and relive the impact of radio, comic strips, and movies on this nation. (Fig. 1, 2, 3)

Games appeal to a great overlapping segment of the collecting field. Aviation, train, and automobile buffs, as well as those infatuated with baseball or art and advertising, all look for appropriate games to fill out their respective collections. While the older games may not be as plentiful as they once were, there are many examples still to be found from the turn of the century through the 1930's and '40's to challenge the searcher. (Fig. 4)

The prices of the games in this book are derived from personal buying experience, auctions, and observing the going rates at shops and antiques shows. To use the well worn phrase—the listed prices are only a guide. Condition, size, rarity, completeness, and even the geography of where you are buying, all serve as important factors in governing prices. Everything considered, however, the end result is always how much an avid game collector is willing to pay to add a desirable game to his or her collection.

The game brings to its buyer beauty, enjoyment, and a distinct sense of history. Without doubt, it's "all in the game."

Fig. 1

Fig. 3

Fig. 2

Fig. 4

ACKNOWLEDGMENTS

I am indebted to the late Edward P. Parker of Parker Brothers, Inc., who so graciously opened that company's archives to me as a neophyte collector.

Also, I am grateful for the friendship and shared knowledge of Herbert Siegel, fellow game collector.

To Harry L. Rinker, my understanding and meticulous editor, goes my appreciation for his help and communication, which knew no limits. He promised during the writing of this book I would become re-acquainted with my own collection and love it more. He was right.

I wish to give sincere thanks to Bruce Whitehill, "The Big Game Hunter," who very generously allowed games from his collection to be photographed.

And last, but certainly not least, I deeply value the constant support of my husband, Rally, who capably doubles as a press agent and always manages to make the space for one more game.

Lee Dennis

GAMES:
PASTIMES OF HISTORY

ANCIENT GAMES

King Tut certainly did not possess a Monopoly board, but he thought enough of the board with which he played to be buried with it. The tomb of Tutankhamen revealed a gaming board, several sets of men, and some dice. Little is recorded of the games the ancients played or how, but doubtlessly games have accompanied civilizations for centuries. They mirror more than any other antique the customs and culture of the people who played them.

Backgammon-like boards found in what is now Iran (Ur of Chaldee in Biblical times) date back at least 4,000 years. Emperor Claudius not only played this style game as "tabula," he also wrote a book on the game. The Romans brought "tabula" to England during their invasion. Logically enough, the English first called the game "tables." Like so many classic games, backgammon probably did not begin as an invention, but as an evolution. Many games have circled our globe and ended up played in various countries, under diverse names, and even in different centuries.

The English played checkers under the name of "draughts," although the Greeks and Romans already had played this game. The French knew it, and still do, as "Jeu de Dames."

Of checkers, Plato once wrote, "the toiling millions raising the Pyramids, the skilled artisans erecting King Solomon's Temple, the heroes of Troy's immortal fame, the conquering hosts of Alexander and Caesar, all enlivened their labors by Draughts. It flourished all these long ages and survived the existence of the greatest nations the world has ever seen, and in one form or another still continues to be a favorite diversion in every corner of the earth."

Some historians believe checkers predates chess; others believe the game is derived from chess. Proof of either claim does not exist, as time and antiquity have clouded their origins. Perhaps India has the edge on chess' longevity. Indians played it prior to 600 A.D. as "chaturanga." "Chatur" meant four and "anga" was a unit of the army. The game undoubtedly followed trade routes to Europe. Unlike any other game,

7

chess enjoyed the sanction of every major religion through the ages because it contained no element of luck or chance. Today, chess collectors seek ornate and unusual sets in ivory, teak, marble, sterling silver, and other exotic media.

Cribbage, a comparative newcomer in 1620, was the brainchild of Sir John Suckling, a British poet. However, the game resembles a much earlier one known as Niddy-Noddy.

Italian monks of the 18th century amused themselves with dominoes, although it is virtually certain that the tiles found their way to Europe from a much earlier Asian source, presumably China. The possibility is strong that dominoes originally were flattened dice.

Fox and Geese, a jumping game played with marbles or pegs, puzzled the English as far back as the 15th century. The basic strategy involved the geese, who could move only in one direction, trying to pen the fox, who could move in any direction. Gradually the game evolved to a solitaire of jumping until just one marble remained on the board, a feat sometimes accomplished, but then not remembered without recording the solution.

Lotto, or as the Germans spelled it, "Loto," was first played in Genoa in the 17th century and often bore colorful lithography on the numbered cards. For many years the game contained small, sharp-edged glass markers, which certainly would not pass the safety standards for children today. Most lotto games came in an assortment of simulated trunk designs. Companies made them in various sizes. (Fig. 5)

The Chinese lay claim to mah-jongg, a highly complicated game with 144 tiles and many other components. Like chess, mah-jongg collectors vie for the more ornate sets made of ivory and stored in handsome, intricately constructed, brass-bound boxes.

A sophisticated form of tic-tac-toe, *Nine Men's Morris* continues to be played in certain parts of the world, particularly the Scandinavian countries. A morris board was incised in a Mesopotamian temple approximately 1400 B.C. Shakespeare mentioned this game in *A Midsummer Night's Dream.* Known by several names, e.g., merels, morelles and mühle, the titles all have the same meaning. "mill." (Fig. 6)

Fig. 5   Fig. 6

8

Perhaps *Parcheesi* possesses the most glamorous background. The national game of India, *Pachisi* derives its name from the Indian word for "twenty-five." The Emperor Akbar in the 16th century laid out the game on a huge marble courtyard. For his playing pieces he used slave girls from his harem dressed in appropriate colors. They moved about the board as each throw of the cowrie shells (used as dice) demanded. Later, the English introduced the game under the name *Ludo*.

The English also gave the world Edmond Hoyle. To this day, doing anything "according to Hoyle" means doing it correctly. Born in 1692, Hoyle taught Londoners the professional way to play the fashionable games of his day, including Whist, the forerunner of Bridge. He wrote several books, and bastardized "Hoyle" books still are teaching games to the public today. Hoyle first popularized the word "score" to indicate the record of a game. His love for games gave him a zest for life that lasted 97 years.

EARLY AMERICAN GAMES

Of course, the early settlers of America brought these games and others, or at least their concepts, across the ocean with them. However, the rigors of carving out a hardscrabble existence in the new world left little time for leisure. Religious scruples played their part, too. The Puritans denounced any form of "pagan merriment." After all, they even had opposed the celebration of Christmas. The magistrates frowned on what they termed the "Sports of the Innyard." They passed specific laws against gaming, viewed dice as "instruments of the devil," and deemed cards as "the devil's picture books."

One of several games they outlawed was that of *Nine Pins*, a bowling game with the pins placed in the formation of a diamond. Our crafty forebears circumvented the ruling by merely adding a pin, placing them in the shape of a triangle and then calling the game *Ten Pins*, which is bowling as we know it today.

The Dutch of New Amsterdam enjoyed more leniency in their lives and played skittles, another form of bowling. Skittles was played on an indoor alley in their taverns. They also amused themselves with *Tick-Tack*, a game greatly resembling backgammon, and *Trock*, a type of indoor croquet played on a table.

Southern colonists, on the other hand, found more time for relaxation, no doubt because of the kinder climate, and greatly indulged in horse racing, gambling, and card playing. Artifacts excavated in Jamestown, Virginia, included ivory fragments of dice and chessmen, and many of Jamestown's 17th century fireplace tiles of Dutch Delft show quaint pictures of children playing skittles, spinning tops, and enjoying other diversions.

By the early 1700's, Ben Franklin recorded games and toys as being advertised and sold in Boston. Franklin also believed that "games lubricate the body and the mind." Yet, never ending chores in our early work-oriented culture found the average American family combining its pleasures with work activities that involved group effort, such as log rollings, corn husking parties, quilting bees, and barn raisings. Except in affluent homes with house servants, taking the time to play a game for the sheer pleasure of it was an infrequent occurrence.

What changed all this? The Industrial Revolution certainly was an instrumental factor. Very gradually, families started to have more time for recreation, and attitudes toward playing games slowly changed. Still, the earliest card and board games of the 19th century reeked with both simplicity and morality. If Americans were to finally unleash their desires for game play, piety was the path by which to do it.

Teetotums (top-like devices with numbers) and later, spinners advanced the play to avoid the use of dice so strongly associated with gambling. Spaces on boards bore labels of honesty and thievery, truthfulness and perjury, and happiness and jail. Players see-sawed between good and evil, always with righteousness as the ultimate goal. Boring and over simplified by today's standards, the 1840's games, many of which were copies of earlier English ones, sought to uplift and moralize.

AMERICAN GAME COMPANIES

One of the first companies to manufacture games in the United States was the W. & S. B. Ives Company of Salem, Massachusetts, established in 1830. In the early nineteenth century, games often were a side line within the province of a stationer or bookseller, rather than a toy manufacturer. The Ives Brothers were well respected stationers. They published several card games, including an old-time favorite, *Dr. Busby*, known in England as *Happy Families*. Anne W. Abbott, daughter of a Beverly, Massachusetts, clergyman, devised this American version. The Ives Company also issued her board games of *Mansion of Happiness* in 1843 and *Reward of Virtue* in 1850. Abbott did not put her name on many of the games, but in some cases the signature would simply state "By a Lady." (Fig. 7)

Fig. 7

Fig. 9

Fig. 8

Ives Brothers lithographed their games in great detail. They were hand painted. Each board folded together, buckled with a strap, and a pouch within the buckle held the gaming pieces. The company also brought out a game with the staggering title, *The Game of Pope or Pagan or the Missionary Campaign or the Siege of the Stronghold of Satan by the Christian Army.* By 1884, both Ives brothers had died. In 1887 the newly formed George S. Parker & Co. acquired the rights to the Ives' games and reissued many of them.

Stationers, much broader in their scope of merchandise than their title indicated, produced all manner of card games, rebuses, geographical cards, cards of Biblical scripture, as well as "guesses" or riddles, and conversation and grammar cards. They also produced maps, dissected and sliced puzzles, and one-time games for an individual inventor.

Other games of this period, the early 1840's, included another tongue twister by L. I. Cohen & Co., card manufacturers of Philadelphia, called *The National Game of the Star Spangled Banner or Geographical and Historical Tour Through the United States and Canada.* Following this patriotic bent, William Chauncey Langdon of New Orleans issued *The Game of American Story and Glory* in 1846.

McLoughlin Brothers

The McLoughlin Brothers, whose father had established a printing firm as early as 1828 in New York City, were active in the production of children's books, puzzles, paper dolls, and blocks. By the 1850's, the concern started to publish a plethora of juvenile games with characters and figures heavily "borrowed" from European neighbors, England and Germany.

As time progressed, the brothers, always on top of new improvements in printing techniques, quickly adopted new processes to their own line. As a result, their chromolithography far outstripped that of their competitors.

Their success enabled them to gradually drop their dependency on pirating foreign material. They cultivated their own stable of American artists, who largely remained anonymous.

McLoughlin Brothers did make games of a religious nature, such as *Pilgrim's Progress* and *Grandmama's Bible Questions.* But, as trends changed and moralistic views relaxed, they published colorful, action-filled board and card games to tempt any child. (Fig. 8)

The large McLoughlin games used wood in their frame construction. Many contained delicate, finely detailed lead figures as their counters. For a very short period, the company employed the beautiful "block" spinners, colorfully lithographed on wood with one or two metal arrows. Eventually, economics led to the use of the more flimsy cardboard spinner.

McLoughlin Brothers relocated several times. These specific addresses help collectors with the dating of McLoughlin games. The company usually dated their work, but not in every instance. They also made and sold labels to some of their competitors.

Since McLoughlin Brothers is so well known for their outstanding lithography, a few words are appropriate on this long overlooked art form. Briefly stated, lithography is a commercial medium for recreating the creative work of others. The early process used flat pieces of limestone on which a special crayon was used to make a drawing. The drawing would attract and hold a greasy ink when it was wet with water. A sheet of paper pressed into contact with the stone then reproduced the drawing. Eventually, technology replaced the limestone with zinc plates. McLoughlin Brothers also pioneered this change. (Fig. 9)

Toward the close of the 19th century, the company's competition narrowed the gap. After John McLoughlin's death in 1905, the heart went out of the business. The sons lacked the verve and vigor of their father. When one son died in 1920, it also was the death knell for the company. Milton Bradley bought the company that same year.

Milton Bradley

Back in 1861, Milton Bradley little realized how the Civil War would change the direction of game playing. At the time, Bradley contributed to the war effort by working as a mechanical draftsman for the Springfield rifle, while stationed at the Armory in Springfield, Massachusetts. Just the year before, his intense interest in the art of lithography had led him to have a lithographic press shipped to Springfield, on which he printed *The Checkered Game of Life,* a game of his own invention. Bradley, the son of a minister, infused his game with religious overtones of vices and virtues, having each player struggle to reach "Happy Old Age" on the fiftieth space. (Fig. 10)

The game sold well for a brief period. When the war started, Bradley closed up his shop and volunteered to work at the Springfield Armory. The town was filled with Union soldiers at the time, and Bradley noticed their boredom and inactivity around the evening campfires. A new idea stirred him into action. Why not develop a game kit for soldiers to while away those vacant hours? He began work on the kit at once. He designed it to be light and small so that it could easily be carried in a pocket or knapsack. Nine games made up the kit—five varieties of dominoes, checkers, chess, backgammon, and, of course, Bradley's own *The Checkered Game of Life.* The kit proved to be an instant hit with the soldiers. Bradley was deluged with orders. By 1865, when the long, dismal conflict came to an end, the entire country yearned for a change of pace. That need would be filled by the "parlor game." Bradley set about seriously to become the "Maker of the World's Best Games."

Most of the Bradley games except for the earlier ones are undated. The four digit serial number found on box covers, always beginning with the number 4, means little. Once a game was discontinued, the company placed the same number on a new game. The company used three signatures: first Milton Bradley & Co., next Milton Bradley Company, and last, Milton Bradley Co. Frequently, the only clue to date rests with the cover design. One needs to study the dress, the event pictured, and other factors to determine an approximate year of manufacture.

An early game of Milton Bradley involved a character named *Sam Slick.* Based on a true figure, Slick was a peddler who traveled through New England and Canada selling clocks. Sam Slick's wise sayings and sly dealings tickled the humor of our forefathers, for Sam Slick personified the type of peddler so familiar at that time on the American scene. (Fig. 11)

Bradley, an avid game player, taught his neighbors a couple of his personal favorites. *Poetical Pot Pie* and *Halma* (1880), which was based on an early Indian game. He always believed that "learning should be fun." Not only did he gear his educational games this way, but the Milton Bradley Company became equally well-known for their kindergarten teaching aids and school supplies. Bradley died in 1911, long before his company was to reach its full potential. (Fig. 12)

Fig. 10

Fig. 11

Fig. 12

Fig. 13

Selchow and Righter

Following the Civil War, a small business owned by Albert J. Swift opened its door on John Street in New York City, as a wholesale distributor for toys and games. In his first catalog of 1867, the game of *Parcheesi* first appeared. In 1870, Swift sold out to Elisha G. Selchow, a paper box jobber at the time. In the changeover, Selchow kept on John H. Righter, a young man who had been working for Swift, and placed him in charge of the new enterprise. Righter managed the company with such sparkling efficiency that Selchow decided to make him a full partner.

The firm registered the name of *Parcheesi* with the patent office in 1874, giving this game one of the earliest trademarks. Although copied by numerous other game companies under different names, such as *Bombay* and *India, Parcheesi* outsold all other board games until *Monopoly* appeared. For many years Selchow and Righter continued to operate as jobbers, handling toys, banks, and games, but *Parcheesi* remained their classic big seller.

Later, Selchow and Righter sold a little puzzle called *Pigs in Clover*, which Charles M. Crandall invented in 1889. President Benjamin Harrison was portrayed in a newspaper cartoon in the White House trying to solve this maddening thing. The media quickly seized the opportunity to ridicule Harrison's attention to pigs instead of serious matters of state. (Fig. 13)

When Righter died in 1909, the company, known by then as the largest jobber of toys and games in the country, decided to incorporate. After Elisha Selchow's death in 1915, the second generation took over. In 1927, Selchow and Righter discontinued its jobbing operation to concentrate on its own line of games. They produced *Fascination,* a marble game played with a top, *Hares and Hounds* and others. Still, it remained for their venerable *Parcheesi* to pull the company through the storms of the Great Depression, when so many other game companies bit the economic dust.

Parker Brothers

Over a century ago, a small game launched a young man into a career which would make his hometown the "Game Capital of the World." George S. Parker utilized his profits from selling produce from his family's garden in Salem, Massachusetts, to publish a card game he called *Banking*. Only 16 years old, he prevailed upon an understanding high school principal to giving him a leave of absence to try and sell the 500 games in the New England area. His success with the sales netted him $100, with which he set up his own company in 1883. His brother joined him in 1888, and the firm became Parker Brothers. George Parker's fervid love of the board game led him to invent over 100 of his company's games before his death in 1953.

Parker spent hours playing games with friends, family, and employees. Some he played over and over in order to iron out difficulties in the rules or scoring. Small wonder that the Parker Brothers games became known for the "excellence of their actual playing qualities." The Parker games won the Highest Award in the World's Columbian Exposition of 1893.

Of all the games George Parker fathered, his favorite was *Chivalry,* a complex game he had worked on even before *Banking*. He claimed it was "the best game in 2,000 years," more complicated than checkers, but not as difficult as chess. Unfortunately, the public did not agree. Many years later, in 1930, he reissued the same game, with a few new rules, different packaging, and the name of *Camelot*. This version topped the popularity chart for games for years after. (Fig. 14)

The company incorporated in 1901. The "Inc." after their name helps a collector identify an undated Parker game as nineteenth or twentieth century.

Parker also enlisted the help of Jasper H. Singer of New York City, who was heavily into the toy and novelty field. Parker offered to be sales agent for Singer in the six New England states. In return, Singer agreed to take on the Parker games as part of his own line. Whether this arrangement had anything to do with it or not, the Parker games and those of the Singer company through the 1890's looked quite similar as to their lithography.

COMMON GAMES

In the era before stringent copyright laws, companies plagiarized from one another. They also produced thousands of common games that were within the public domain. *Authors* supposedly was invented by August A. Smith in the 1860's, with the aid of his students at a Salem seminary. Churches considered the card game an educational tool to learn culture. Many sponsored "Authors" socials. Members rejoiced learning who wrote the best sellers of the day, without necessarily having to read them. Periodically updated as new authors made the literary scene, the game flourished well into the 20th century. Other games suffering much the same overkill included *Jack Straws, Fish Pond, Peter Coddles* (who seemed to take trips everywhere), *Tiddledy Winks,* and *Old Maid.* These games because of their tremendous numbers do not interest advanced collectors. However, some card buffs do seek out different Old Maids. (Fig. 15)

Old Maid was relatively unknown outside of America. Invariably the pairs of cards reflected this country's social structure at the time each *Old Maid* was published. Producers of the game constantly revamped the characters in dress and expression to fit the period. The Old Maid herself saw little change, always being spinsterish in looks, with spectacles and oftentimes with a cat, parrot, or a cup of tea.

Fig. 14

Fig. 15

Three other very common games belong to Parker Brothers. The huge popularity of *Pit, Rook* and *Flinch* have resulted in an available abundance of these card games today. *Flinch* originally was produced by the Flinch Card Company of Kalamazoo, Michigan, makers also of *Bourse* and *Roodles*. The company sold out to Parker Brothers in 1936.

By the end of the nineteenth century, games symbolized home entertainment. Entire families gathered around their dining room table to indulge in a bit of frivolity, whether it be *Table Croquet* or *Fish Pond*. Many families were likely to treasure their games so that they would last through several generations. Often, some attentive adult preserved a well used game by applying neat, strong herringbone stitching to splitting box seams to hold them together. (Fig. 16)

Fig. 16

NEW THEMES

Games gradually stopped emphasizing morality and reached out in other directions, mainly educating while also being amusing. "Education by Play," a booklet which described the offerings of the Cincinnati Game Company of Ohio, advertised a full range of educational card games from *Mythology* to *Wild Animals*. The Knapp Electric Novelty and Toy Company of Port Chester, New York, introduced in 1894 one of the first educational games operated by battery, *Bell of Fortune*. It mechanically rang a bell for the correct answer to a keyed question.

Besides offering educational value, games made a social comment on life as it was.

Milton Bradley's *A Sheaf of Wheat,* which traced the gripping history of a loaf of bread from wheat field to bake shop, would not be too exciting, perhaps, to *Trivial Pursuit* buffs of the 1980's. Repugnant to today's players also would be the prejudicial activities symbolized by the game theme of *Alabama Coon* or *Little Black Sambo*. (Fig. 17)

Glorifying this nation's conflict were the myriad of Spanish-American war games, from Parker Brothers' board game, *The Siege of Havana,* to Selchow and Righter's card game of *Admiral Dewey,* to McLoughlin Brothers' puzzle, *Up the Heights of San Juan.*

Entire families stung their fingers on *Crokinole,* a sort of hand shuffleboard, or made fools of themselves over a hilarious balloon game of Parker Brothers, called *Pillow-Dex.* No matter what the subject, games were here to stay. (Fig. 18)

Fig. 17

Fig. 18

TWENTIETH CENTURY CLASSICS

Following the turn of the century, new classics emerged. George S. Parker bought from England the American rights to the popular game of table tennis and coined the name *Ping-Pong* from the sound of the celluloid ball being struck by the paddle and then hitting the table. By 1902, *Ping-Pong* was the national rage. Dining room tables enjoyed a new use as *Ping-Pong* courts. (Fig. 19)

Fig. 19

World War I induced another spate of war games. In 1915, Parker Brothers brought out *Pollyanna,* the "glad game." Based on a best selling book of the time, Pollyanna, the heroine, managed to find good in every adversity. Her adventures lent themselves well to a board game. Pollyanna's popularity so endured that Parker Brothers updated the game from time to time in hair style and dress. Selchow and Righter's *Parcheesi* chugged along steadily. (Fig. 20)

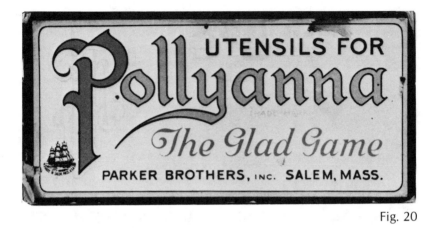

Fig. 20

Milton Bradley scored an enormous success in 1918 with their game *Uncle Wiggily,* based on the exploits of a long eared rabbit. Howard R. Garis wrote the humorous series of stories, which delighted children and adults alike.

When Garis first conceived his *Uncle Wiggily* game, he had been unwrapping some meat from his butcher. On impulse, he took the blood-stained wrapping paper and roughly sketched on it the track for *Uncle Wiggily.* Soon after, he visited the Milton Bradley offices and challenged one of their representatives to a game. Garis lost the game, but sold the idea to Milton Bradley, butcher paper and all. The company published it for years afterward.

Through this era, the lithography on the game covers grew flatter and much less detailed. By the 1920's, graphics had changed perceptibly. Colors were brighter than ever, but the pizzazz was gone.

About this time, people began talking about pung and chow, bamboos, flowers, and seasons. The craze of *Mah-Jongg* hit the country. Chief exponent of the game was Joseph P. Babcock, a Standard Oil representative stationed in Soochow, China, at the close of World War I. He often had watched the Chinese play it. He simplified the rules for western play, brought the game to San Francisco, and arranged to have Parker Brothers handle the sales. *Mah-Jongg* boomed. While the name was duly registered, other game companies escaped this thorny issue by manufacturing sets of their own, but calling them *Pe-Ling, Pung-Chow, The Chinese Game,* and a host of other aliases.

A "talking board" and its wandering planchette spellbound believers during this same period. The *Ouija* board, invented several years earlier by toy manufacturers William and Isaac Fuld of Baltimore, finally caught on with the public. The board, a fabulous fad, or fraud as some insisted, caused more comment than the weather. Advocates consulted their *Ouija* boards (the name is a combination of the French and German words for "yes") in preference to their own bankers, doctors, and lawyers. The demand for the board died out as suddenly as it began, only to be revived about 50 years later by its new owners, Parker Brothers. (Fig. 21)

Lindbergh's historic flight across the Atlantic in 1927 inspired numerous games: three by Parker Brothers, one of which was *Lindy*; *Flight to Paris* by Milton Bradley; and, *Ski-Hi* by Cutler and Saleeby, just to name a few.

The movies, radio, and comic strips popularized a galaxy of games. *Movieland Keeno,* published by Wilder of St. Louis, *The Talking Picture Game* as well as the comic characters, *The Nebbs, Ella Cinders,* and *Andy Gump* all by Milton Bradley, *Radio Game* by Alderman Fairchild, and Parker Brothers' *Eddie Cantor and Tell It to the Judge, Baron Munchausen,* and *Ed Wynn* constituted only a small portion of the entertainment and celebrity games which were marketed. (Fig. 22-24)

Classic books like *Tom Sawyer, The Wizard of Oz, Winnie the Pooh,* and several others became board games. Milton Bradley issued *Sorry* and *Go to the Head of the Class,* both of which are near classics today.

Fig. 21

Fig. 22

Fig. 23

Fig. 24

Monopoly

Parker Brothers first listed adult games in 1931. In 1935, they brought out a game that set all records for the industry. The timing, during the Great Depression, was right; whole families took to this huge seller, *Monopoly.* Who could resist *Monopoly's* concept of making a fortune when all over the country people were entering bankruptcy?

When Monopoly was originally presented to Parker Brothers, the company turned the game down unanimously. Why? They claimed it had 52 fundamental errors, which boiled down to the game being too long, too complicated, and too expensive to make.

Eventually, Parker Brothers decided to produce the game. The game of Monopoly skyrocketed and eventually sold over 80 million sets. It was published in at least 14 different languages. It first appeared from Parker Brothers just before Christmas of 1935. Orders poured in to Parker Brothers from all over the country. Their files overflowed, and back orders ended up stowed in large laundry baskets along the corridors. As one man said at the time, "It looks like Parker Brothers is taking in washing."

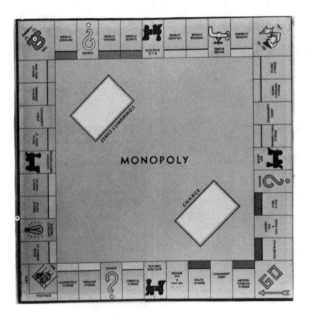

Fig. 25

Disney

During this time, Walt Disney was putting together an empire with a mouse and a duck. Mickey Mouse, Donald Duck, and later The Three Little Pigs and the Big Bad Wolf, Snow White and the Seven Dwarfs, and other Disney enterprises found themselves subjects for games. (Fig. 26)

Fig. 26

NEW COMPANIES AND MERGERS

New companies appeared on the game horizon: Rosebud Art Co., who sold the ever popular Popeye, Transogram, E. S. Lowe (later sold to Milton Bradley), and J. Pressman & Co. Although it must be admitted that these companies did not put the workmanship into their games as those of the established game manufacturers, they all competed for the Depression dollar.

The large game companies continue to turn out game successes, although some things have changed. Selchow & Righter, formerly of Bay Shore, Long Island, once claimed they were the oldest family-owned game concern. Now, this company is owned by Hasbro/Milton Bradley. Milton Bradley has been absorbed by Hasbro Toys of Pawtucket, Rhode Island. Parker Brothers recently was purchased by Hasbro Toys.

LOST COMPANIES

Yet what happened to the old game companies of Clark and Sowdon, West and Lee, Noyes and Snow, C. H. Joslin, Stoll and Edwards, and so many others? Little information exists on the majority of them. They could have ceased publishing because of fire, flood, bankruptcy, or buy-outs by other companies. Catalogs from most have failed to surface. Their disappearance presents a challenging search to the game collector.

GAME CATEGORIES

Despite the huge numbers of games, the game playing methodology, like literature plots, vary very little. Game experts categorize them into four or five slots. These are known by different names, such as position or opposition games, which can be broadly defined as strategy games. This obviously includes chess, checkers, and other similar types.

By far, the most common is the race or track game, where players vie to be the first to reach a designated goal. A parcheesi-type board often is involved. Games of skill encompass ball and cup, target games, tiddledy winks, and many others. Educational games comprise a fourth type of play. (Fig. 27-32)

The more complex and absorbing games combine at least two and sometimes three of these basic plays. *Monopoly* is a good example of this.

Fig. 27

Fig. 28

Fig. 29

Fig. 30

Fig. 31

Fig. 32

MODERN GAMES AND COLLECTORS

Besides mirroring the modes and mores of our nation, games criss-cross in different directions to different collectors. The railroad addict certainly desires the stunning graphics of the game *Train to Boston,* for the same reasons aviation devotees seek out a game like *Flying the U. S. Air Mail,* or baseball fans an early game of *Base-Ball.* Animal collectors are attracted to covers of cats, pigs, mice, horses, and various breeds of dogs. (Fig. 33-36)

The type of dog often helps to date a cover, as different breeds of dogs were associated with certain eras. The Saint Bernard frequently appeared in games from the 1890's, the bulldog through the 1920's, and the Scotch terrier, popularized by F.D. Roosevelt's *Fala,* in the 1930's.

Fig. 33

SCROLL·PUZZLE

Fig. 34

Fig. 35

Fig. 36

In addition, art-related covers e.g., Santa Claus, fire fighters, and policemen, appeal to segments of the collecting world, besides just the collector of games. (Fig. 37, 38)

Games have evolved into more sophisticated forms. The simple anagram letter game developed to *Probe, Scrabble, Boggle,* and other modern spelling games. *Jack Straws* emerged again in the 1930's as the very popular *Pick-Up-Sticks. Chinese Checkers* grew from the old game of *Halma,* and *Lotto* became *Keno* and then *Bingo.* (Fig. 39, 40)

Games continue to express the way we live. In recent years the public has played *Watergate, Guru, Headache, The Safety Belt Game,* and *Ulcers*—certainly a reflection of our culture of the 1970's and 1980's. This is why the games people play always will become fascinating boxes of history.

Fig. 37

Fig. 38

Fig. 39

Fig. 40

HOW TO COLLECT GAMES

Games, while rising steadily in value, have not reached the astronomic prices of some other items, e.g., dolls and toys. Although old games still are plentiful, the old adage holds true: "buy quality, not quantity."

Condition is everything, especially in this field where you are dealing with a great deal of cardboard and paper that have been children's playthings for many years. The only time you forgive questionable condition (and then only a little!) is when a game is exceedingly old or rare, and you have that feeling you may never see the likes of it again.

Graphics on the cover take high priority in the purchase of a game. Also, any cover picture that deals with unusual or highly collectible subject matter (e.g., Santa Claus) presents a desirable buy.

Size plays a part, too. Generally speaking, the larger the game, the more value it has.

Completeness certainly is important, especially the instructions. When you come across games that are badly ripped and flattened catastrophes beyond redemption, always save what collectors term the "guts" of the game. These include the counters, spinners, dice, figures, and directions. Maintaining a stockpile of these old parts enables you to complete a game that is missing its pieces, but otherwise is in good condition.

Auctions occasionally sell games. But, as with any other auction merchandise, a preview inspection is essential. Flea markets often sell games. If the market is an outdoor one, exercise caution. Prime examples of games rarely are found at an outdoor market. The extremes of temperature and weather as well as careless handling often produce "rough" games. Doll, toy, and ephemera shows are much better sources for games in good condition.

"Games in good shape never bear tape." Any type of tape is an anathema to a game collector. No matter how carefully you try to remove it, the lithography of the cover or the paper covering the sides of the box will come off with the tape. Never repair with tape. A good conservator's glue is far better. If a price tag has been thoughtlessly stickered to the face of the game's cover, forget about buying it at any price.

In your quest for games, be alert to what people tell you about them. This holds equally true when people view your own collection. Many worthwhile tidbits of information can be gleaned this way. Someone who played the game years ago or is familiar with the game company is a key source. It is not beyond the realm of possibility to run into a former archivist of a game company, to hear a former chauffeur relate his experiences in the employ of a games executive, or to learn that the seller of your game had a favorite great-uncle who once was an illustrator for Parker Brothers. Little segments of game history like these are priceless, since records of most companies are incomplete at best, if not gone forever.

By all means, keep a games inventory. Name, manufacturer, year, size, some description, and what you paid for it are invaluable for your own information as well as for insurance or appraisal purposes. Computers make keeping an inventory easy these days. A well kept notebook that you can carry with you also will serve your purpose. You will be surprised in your search for games how easily you can forget the ones you already have.

Naturally, this does not apply if you are buying a game to replace one you already have. A serious collector always tries to upgrade his or her collection. Moreover, the true collector studies and reads everything available on the subject of games and keeps files on this information. To collect is also to learn.

HOW TO DISPLAY A GAME COLLECTION

As with most collections, the greatest satisfaction comes from enjoying the games visually. Well displayed, games provide an insight into another era of time.

The chromolithography on the box covers of games intrigues the majority of game collectors, not the game play. To be sure, the inside boards also may warrant notice. But, by and large, the boards of most games frequently do not measure up to the expectations generated by the cover.

If the cover is dirty with dust or soot, take a soft sponge and with warm water and Ivory soap, gently clean the cover *only*. The lithography is very durable and usually cleans up well. But, be careful. If you wet the cardboard sides, they will absorb the moisture and weaken the structure of the cover. If desired, you then can spray a thin coat of clear lacquer on just the cover top. This will keep it bright and easy to dust.

Now that you have your games clean and presentable, how can you display them? You can take one room and build shelves for each wall. Keep the shelving in line with good visibility. In other words, do not have them flush to the floor or close to the ceiling. On the back of each shelf games can be set on their side edges to show the cover. Other games can be placed flat in front of the standing ones.

Another method requires installing peg board. This arrangement can extend from floor to ceiling. Each game rests on the metal peg board hooks, which can vary in width to accommodate the size of each game. However, this technique does require that many of the games be secured. Otherwise, the box covers fall forward and the game components drop out. You can tie them with a light bakery-type string or use rubber bands. The rubber bands should be selected in different sizes to the proportion of each game to eliminate rubbing. Use two on opposite ends, close to the game border, to avoid detracting from the cover picture.

If you have no room to display your games, do not wrap them in plastic envelopes or sheeting for any length of time, as they cannot breathe. If games must be stacked, do not place more than three on top of one another. The accumulation of weight is damaging. Use a sheet of acid-free paper between each box to help in preservation.

Sunlight warps boxes and fades colors. Keep games away from sunny areas. A long center hallway often becomes an ideal area to display games. Extremes of heat are very damaging, attested to by anyone who has found brittle games with "dished in" covers long stored in an attic. Moisture is equally ruinous. Avoid damp basements for a game collection. Games are a form of ephemera and must be treated accordingly.

Framing games is an expensive alternative. Some purists feel it lowers the value of a game to place it behind glass. The collector has to make his or her own decision here. If just the cover exists and it has great color and good graphics, framing is an excellent route to preserve that which is not complete anyway.

Likewise, framing a very old game board that you are not likely to come across again is acceptable, providing the framer uses all the conservation techniques, such as acid-free matting, spacers, etc. But to frame each complete game, with open box, open board and the gaming pieces would be costly, indeed, and consume a good deal of wall space.

Besides using games as wall decorations, many collectors prefer to display them in groupings with other collections. Games certainly complement a toy or doll collection. If a collector focuses on the primitive, painted wooden gameboards, these blend well with early country items and are right at home with a quilt collection.

ANTIQUE AMERICAN GAMES

ABINGTON PRESS

New York, NY; Cincinnati, OH

ca 1920's

Bible Game of Facts, Places, and Events, card game, 1922, 3 x 3½", 64 cards and instruction booklet, backs show map of Palestine, invented by Josephine L. Baldwin **10.00**

ADAMS & CO.

Boston, MA

ca 1860's

Mixed Pickles, card game, 1867, 3 x 4½", 90 pieces [30 red cards, 30 white cards, 30 blue cards], no illustrations on cards, directions on back of box cover **35.00**

C. E. AKINS

ca 1890's

Parlor Quoits, skill, ©1891, 12 x 7", 18 pieces [11 x 11" felt with target in red and yellow, 12 celluloid quoits, 4 propelling celluloid disks, and instruction sheet], similar to *Tiddledy Winks* **40.00**

AKRO AGATES

Clarksburg, WV   1932-51

Click, ca 1930's, 7½ x 7½ x 1", marble game, ················· **25.00**

Kings, 1931, 11 x 7⅛ x ⅞", marble game ···················· **30.00**

ALDERMAN-FAIRCHILD
(ALL—FAIR)

Churchville, NY; Rochester, NY   1920-40's

Fairchild bought out Alderman. Company was located in Churchville, New York, until 1935. Games trademarked ALL—FAIR.

Cities, card game, 1932, 5 x 4 x 1", No. 428, each card spells part of the name of U.S. city ·········· **25.00**

Flap Jacks, skill, ©1931, 15½ x 12½", 10 pieces, all flap jacks, which are tossed into 5 numbered round holes of beige, blue and red board, directions on back of box cover ············· **35.00**

Game of Poor Jenny, The, boxed board game, ©1927, 11½ x 11½", 9 pieces [4 metal donkeys, 4 wooden cubes, cardboard playing board], directions on back of box cover, board marked off in squares, with pictures of donkeys and Black Mammy figures **65.00**

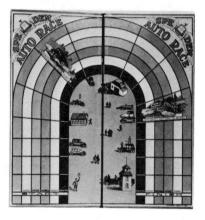

Spedem Auto Race, separate board and pieces box, patented April 20, 1922, 17 x 17½", multicolored, folding board of race track, 4½ x 3¾" box with 14 pieces [dice cup, 6 wooden dice, 6 metal cars, and instruction sheet], cars are different colors and labeled Saxon, Dodge, Maxwell, Paige, Ford and Buick **95.00**

Toonin Radio Game, separate board and pieces box, ca 1910's, game board 17¼ x 17 ⅝", 6 metal speakers [tokens], 6 wood cubes, instruction sheet, dice cup, board shows call letters for radio stations **95.00**

Spedem Junior Auto Race Game, boxed board game, ©1928,, 11½ x 11½",
No. 407, 4 playing pieces [4 metal cars],
directions on back of cover, cardboard
race track, multicolored, with 3½"
spinner in center, set into box bottom,
car spaces named Ford, Buick, Stutz
and Dodge **110.00**

Wyntre Golf **120.00**

**Way To The White House, The, Game
of Electing The President,** 1927, 15½
x 12", No. 304 . . . . **55.00**

X-Plor US, separate board and pieces
box, ca 1922, 17½ x 17½" game board,
5¾ x 4" pieces box, No. 3, 5 pieces [4
metal airplanes and score pad], orange
board has multicolored lithographed
map of U.S., directions printed on bottom in center **85.00**

THE AMERICAN TOY AIRSHIP CO.

Mansfield, OH · ca 1920's

Mumbly Peg, skill, ca 1920's, $7\frac{3}{8}$ x $7\frac{1}{2}$ x $\frac{7}{8}$", 32 pieces [target, 21 wooden pegs, 4 round felt pads, 5 rings, 1 snapper], instructions printed on side of box lid, 4 color round target with center plus 4 rings **20.00**

AMERICAN TOY WORKS

New York, NY · ca 1930's

Aero-Chute Target Game, $19\frac{3}{16}$ x $13\frac{3}{16}$ x $2\frac{1}{8}$", 8 pieces [3 airplanes, 2 parachutists, game board of sky and target, dowel, dart] **60.00**

Library of Games [Chess, Checkers, Chunga, Merelles, Py-hy-ky, Tigh, Avion, Yumph, Foregammon, and others], 1938, 16 x $12\frac{1}{4}$ x $1\frac{3}{4}$", No. 403, 2 game boards, numerous chess and checker style pieces, 16 pegs, $4\frac{5}{16}$ x 5" instruction book **25.00**

BAKER & BENNETT CO.
(American Novelties)

New York, NY

Psychology of The Hand, $8\frac{3}{4}$ x $12\frac{1}{4}$ x $1\frac{1}{2}$", copyrighted by Gertrude Ann Lindsay, 5 cards of hands, each divided into character sections, instruction booklet **35.00**

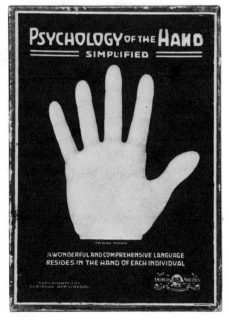

BEACON HUDSON COMPANY

Boston, MA   ca 1920's

Open Championship Golf Game, boxed board game, ca 1925, 13 x 19", directions on back of box cover, multicolor board on cardboard box bottom shows yardages of "links" and has six attached spinners each labeled 'brassie', 'niblick', driver, etc. **120.00**

FREDERICH H. BEACH

New York, NY   ca 1930's

Four Games [Noodle Soup, 2nd Series; Scrambles, 11th Series; Scrambles, 12th Series; Wordlets, 3rd Series], party or parlor game, 1936, 9 x 11½ x 1⅛", paper sheets **20.00**

BIDDLE CORPORATION

Philadelphia, PA   ca 1910's

Neutral Game of War, Peace and Indemnity, The, card game, 1916, 7¼ x 4", 104 cards and instruction card, card backs are light green and white picturing swords and cannon **25.00**

HARRY S. BIRD

Newark, NJ

Scratch, educational, 10½ x 10½", 2 pieces [spinner and score pad], bottom of box has "Educating Games Co." and instructions, large 10" metal multicolored spinner with hen and basket of eggs, and time tables all around circumference **50.00**

R. BLISS MANUFACTURING CO.

Pawtucket, RI ca 1832-1914

Incorporated in 1873; taken over by Mason & Parker Manufacturing Company, Winchendon, Massachusetts.

Five Little Pigs Puzzle, The, puzzle, ©1888, 6½" square wooden box, "feed trough" glued to bottom of box, 5 clay marbles representing pigs, bottom of box has advertisement for additional Bliss games **55.00**

Game of Balloon, skill, 1889, 31 x 10½", 17 pieces [wooden standard and hoop, 2 racquets (tied like macrame) 4 balloons, 1 inflator, 1 game counter, 4 score pins, instruction booklet advertising sheet], box all wood, dovetailed and hinged **595.00**

THE BOSTON HERALD

Boston, MA ca 1900

Game of Success, The, card game, 2½ x 3", ca 1905-08, 60 cards and instruction sheet, advertising game for *Boston Herald* **40.00**

JOSEPH BORZELLINO & SON

Atlantic City, NJ ca 1930's

Soldier On Fort, The, separate board and pieces box, ©1931, 3¾ x 6¼" box, 17 pieces [gameboard, 14 wood pieces, 2 instruction sheets, advertising sheet], separate instructions, gameboard, strategy, four concentric circles and two forts, military scenes in corners; based on tactics at fort of Verdun in World War I **25.00**

MILTON BRADLEY COMPANY

East Longmeadow, MA   1860

The company's first manufactured game was *The Checkered Game of Life.* Founder Milton Bradley died in 1911, and the reins of the company were assumed by James Shea, Sr. Bradley rarely dated its games, and serial numbers on the games mean little since they were often used for more than one game. Bradley took over McLoughlin Brothers in 1920. The company also produced optical toys and school aids. Bradley was bought by Hasbro Industries, Inc., of Pawtucket, Rhode Island, in 1984.

Across The Yalu, boxed board game, ca 1905, 15 x 9", 13 pieces [12 colored wooden counters and spinner], instructions on back of box cover, multicolored lithographed board shows Yalu River in center with Russians on one bank and Japanese on other; strategy game, unusual subject matter **75.00**

American Boy Game, boxed board game, ca 1924-26, 19 x 9½", 6 pieces [4 round, wooden counters, spinner and board], instructions on back of box cover, multicolored lithographed board folds in half, pictures Boy Scouts in each corner, fleur de lis and "Be Prepared" in center; track game **120.00**

Adventures of the Nebs, boxed board game, ca 1925-27, 19 x 10", 29 pieces [20 colored, numbered wooden counters, 2 dice cups, 2 dice, 4 wooden blocks, board], instructions on back of box cover, board multicolored, lithographed, folds in half; track game patterned after 1920's comic strip, *The Nebs* **75.00**

An Account of Peter Coddles Visit To New York, ca 1890, 5 x 6", numerous printed cards and reading booklet, instructions on back of box cover **20.00**

Auto Race Game, boxed board game, ca 1925, 16⁷/8 x 8¾", 8 pieces [4 ndividual box spinners, 4 colored, metal racing cars], instructions on back of box cover, multicolored lithographed board has black and white checkered race track with driver in race car pictured at upper center, board leaves 2" partition at bottom for playing pieces **195.00**

'Babe' Ruth's Baseball Game, boxed board game, ca 1926-28, 19 x 10", 12 round wooden counters, 85 cards, multicolored lithographed board inserts onto box bottom, instructions on back of box cover, score forms also on back of box cover, autographed, authorized Babe Ruth edition, published in conjunction with Christy Walsh Syndicate **800.00**

Blockade, boxed board game, ca 1898, 7¼ x 7¼", 3 pieces [2 wooden counters and cardboard grid], instructions on back of cover, grid of black and white has red diagonal lines and blue star and is labeled "Harbor" in blue; strategy game reflecting Spanish-American War **20.00**

Bradley's Telegraph Game, educational, ca 1905, 10⁵/8 x 8", pieces include wooden telegraph key, toy money, several telegram blanks, night letter blanks, cablegrams and envelopes, instructions on back of box cover, including Morse code **115.00**

Bradley's Toy Town Post Office, educational, © 1910, 8¼ x 11", 10+ pieces [postman's mask, 2 cardboard sections and 2 wooden supports to create office, stamp, stamp pad, many letters, envelopes, postcards, toy stamps], instructions on back of box cover . . **125.00**

Bull in a China Shop, skill, © 1906, 12" square, 9 pieces [8 wooden tenpins and metal, spring top] instructions on back of box cover, natural wood boxed board has 8 affixed black pegs, and black circles on which to stand pins **40.00**

Columbus, puzzle, patented Dec. 15, 1891, $5^{1}/_{4}$ × $5^{3}/_{4}$", 9 wooden pieces and instruction sheet, with solution to puzzle, wooden box, published for the 400th anniversary of Columbus discovering America **50.00**

Checkered Game of Life, The, framed, 1866, 18" square, red, black, and white lithography on card board; Bradley's first game **800.00**

Cinderella, card game, ca 1900, 6¾ x 5½", 33 cards and instruction card . **20.00**

Cinderella, card game, ca 1921, No. 4111 6¾ x 5½ x 1" **15.00**

Cross Country Marathon **40.00**

Down the Pike with Mrs. Wiggs at the St. Louis Exposition, card game, 1904, 7½ x 5½", instructions in front of reading booklet and many small cards of phrases for reading into the narrative, similar to *Peter Coddles* **15.00**

Easy Money, boxed board game, ca 1935, 19 x 10", 2 dice, several multicolored buildings, 6 wooden counters, 24 cards, instruction sheet, orange, yellow, black and blue board folds in half, track game; believe this to be Bradley's answer to PB's *Monopoly* . . . **25.00**

Excursion to Coney Island, card game, copyrighted, but no date, ca 1885, 4¾ X 3¾" numerous printed cards and reading booklet **20.00**

Fairyland Game, ca 1880's, 11¼ x 11¼ x ⁷⁄₈" **30.00**

Fast Mail, The, ca 1900, $20^5/_8$ x $10^5/_8$", 7 pieces [6 round colored wooden counters and spinner], multicolored lithographed board pictures same train in center as is on cover, wooden box, instructions on back of box cover, track game **800.00**

Fibber McGee, © 1936, 7⁷/₁₆ x 5³/₈ x 1⁵/₈"
No. 4561 . . . . **15.00**

**Fibber McGee and the Wistful Vista
Mystery,** ©1940, 7³/₈ x 5³/₈ x 2",
No. 4768, numerous pieces [150 + 2½
x 10 printed cards, colored disks, 32
page, 4⁷/₈ x 7" story booklet], published
by arrangement with National Broad-
casting Company and Needham,
Louis, & Brorby, Inc. **20.00**

Fire Fighters, boxed board game, ©1909,
8¹/₈ x 14¼", 5 pieces [4 round colored
wooden counters and spinner], instructions printed on face of cover, multicolored lithographed board shows fire
ladders against burning building, with
little girl in window at top . . . **110.00**

Fire Department, ca 1920's, 10¼ x 6¼
x ⁷/₈", 6 pieces [gameboard on bottom
at base, spinner, 4 colored wood chips],
track **25.00**

Flight to Paris, The, boxed board game
©1927, 17 x 8¾", 5 pieces [4 colored
metal planes and spinners], instructions on back of box cover, multicolored lithographed board shows
track across Atlantic Ocean from New
York to Paris with compass in lower
center **160.00**

Flivver Game, separate board and pieces box, ca 1923-24, 16 x 16" board folds in half, matching 6¼ x 4¼" box, 5 playing pieces [4 colored metal cars, and cardboard black and white flivver with moveable wheels that double as spinners] instructions on back of box cover, multicolored track shows old-time cars **195.00**

Game of Advance and Retreat, boxed board game, ca 1900, 19½ × 10¼", 14 round colored wooden markers, instructions on back of box cover, multicolored lithographed board has red and blue checker board surrounded by court pictures, cannon, knights, etc., strategy game . . **145.00**

Fox Hunt, boxed board game, ©1905, 16¼ x 11¼", 6 round colored wooden counters, multicolored lithographed board showing rock wall fence, dog, foxes, instructions on back of box cover, strategy game **50.00**

Game of Air Mail, The, boxed board game, ca 1926-28, 15 x 15", 5 pieces [4 round wooden counters and spinner], instructions on back of box cover, multicolored lithographed board pasted on cardboard insert into box, track game **120.00**

G-Men, card game, 1936, 5½ x 4 x ⅞", No. 4641, Carolyn Wells, writer, 52 cards [4 sets of 12 cards, 1 set of 4 cards], instruction book, uses bidding, trumps, and tricks **30.00**

Game of Air Mail, boxed board game, ca 1927, 12½ x 6¼", 6 marbles and gold and red board with holes for marbles, instructions on back of box cover **45.00**

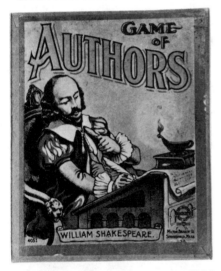

Game of Authors, card game, ca 1890, 5½ x 6¾", 20 cards with red and white flowered backs and faces with black and white lithographed portraits of famous authors, instructions on back of box cover **10.00**

Game of Bear Hunt, boxed board game, ca 1923, 12¼" square, 5 pieces [4 round colored wooden counters and spinner], multicolored lithographed board shows path winding through green countryside, directions printed at bottom of board, track game **60.00**

Game of Fish Pond, The, boxed board game, ca 1895, 21 x 12¾", 2 fishing poles and many numbered fish, instructions on back of box cover, multicolored lithographed board depicts pond with several fish and slots in which to mount loose fish to be caught, wooden box **125.00**

Game of Goat, card game, ©1916, 5½ x 4", 60 cards, red and white backs, red and white faces, and instruction booklet **10.00**

Game of Gypsy Fortune Teller, ca 1922, 6¾ x 5½ x 1″, No. 4271 . . . . . **10.00**

Game of Mail, Express or Accommodation, boxed board game, ©1895, 22 x 14½″, 5 pieces+ [4 round colored wooden markers and spinner] instructions on back of box cover, numerous printed cards, multicolored lithographed board is map of U.S. dated 1894 with railroad routes, right 4½″ of map flips up to reveal game pieces, wooden box; this is an updated 1920's cover of McLoughlin Bros. older game; Bradley re-issued this after buying out McLoughlin in 1920 . . . . **475.00**

Game of Nations, card game, ©1908, 6 x 7½″, 36 multicolored lithographed cards representing nations, instructions on back of box cover **20.00**

Game of Old Mother Hubbard, boxed board game, ca 1890, 15 x 16″, 8 pieces [2 dice cups, 2 dice, 4 round colored wooden counters] instructions on back of box cover, multicolored lithographed board with circle in center representing cupboard, track game . . . **95.00**

Game of Old Mrs. Goose, 9 x 15 x 1³/₁₆″, No. 470 . . . . **30.00**

Game of Siege, skill, ca 1918, 14¼ x 10¼", 35 pieces [metal and wood pistol, 10 wooden "shots", 14 card board soldiers on wooden supports], instructions on back of box cover, target game **140.00**

Game of Spot, boxed board game, ca 1925, 12¼" square, 5 pieces [4 round colored wooden counters and spinner], multicolored lithographed board presents simple track with picture of bulldog in center **40.00**

Game of Signs, The, card game, ca 1890, 5 x 6", 32 multicolored lithographed cards, pertaining to omens and superstitions, instructions on back of box cover **20.00**

Game of Snow White and The Seven Dwarfs, The, boxed board game, ©1937 (Walt Disney Enterprises), 19 x 19½", 54 pieces [2 dice, board, 8 colored wooden counters, 7 dwarf counters, 1 Queen, 1 Huntsman, 1 Poisoned Apple, 28 small multicolored wooden sticks, 4 kiss pieces and instruction sheet], multicolored lithographed board folds in half, track game **120.00**

Game of Steeple Chase, boxed board game, ca 1910, 8¼ x 14¼", 5 pieces [4 round colored wooden markers and spinner], instructions on face of cover, multicolored lithographed board represents oval race track with two horses racing in center **40.00**

Game of Stop, Look and Listen, boxed board game, ca 1926, 14⅛ x 8⅛, 5 pieces [4 round colored wooden counters and spinner], multicolored lithographed board has simple track with instructions printed at top **35.00**

Game of The Stubborn Pig, boxed board game, ca 1910, 15 x 9″, 5 pieces [4 colored wooden counters and spinner], instructions on back of box cover, multicolored lithographed board shows pigs at market in center, with checkered numbered squares around perimeter, track game **50.00**

Game of Tom Sawyer, The, boxed board game, ca 1937, 19 x 10″, 74 pieces [8 colored wooden counters, 2 dice, 14 yellow round disks, 48 cards, instruction sheet and board], multicolored lithographed board folds in half, shows scenes from Tom Sawyer, track game based on movie **75.00**

Game of Three Blind Mice, boxed board game, ca 1925, 9 x 15″, 6 round colored wooden counters, instructions on back of box cover, multicolored lithographed board depicts several mice, cheese, trap, etc., track game **45.00**

Game of The Transatlantic Flight, boxed board game, ca 1924, 21½ x 9¼″, 9 pieces [6 colored metal airplanes, 2 spinners, lift out board] instructions on back of box cover, multicolored lithographed board has accordion fold and opens to 34¼ x 20″, shows map of North Atlantic between Nova Scotia and Great Britain, wooden box **185.00**

Game of Voyage Round the World,
ca 1930's, 16³/₈ x 11⁷/₈ x 1½", No.
4189 . . . . **125.00**

Gypsy Fortune Telling Game, The, boxed board game, ca 1895, 16¼ x 11¾",
7 pieces (black wand, 4 colored wooden counters, lift out board, instruction sheet], multicolored lithographed folded board opens to 23 x 15¾", has playing cards and fortune symbols on green background **75.00**

Go Bang, ca 1890's 8⁷/₈ x 8⁷/₈ x ⁵/₈", No.
4162 . . . . **35.00**

Home History Game, card game, ca
1909, 5⁵/₈ x 6¾", numerous white cards
printed with historical dates, not illustrated, instructions on back of box
cover **20.00**
Grandma's Game of Useful Knowledge,
quiz, ca 1910, 6¼ x 8¼", 101 pieces
[100 cards with questions, instruction
answer book] **20.00**

Honey Bee Game, boxed board game, ca 1913, 12¼" square, 26 pieces [24 round colored metal disks, large revolving metal disk that fits into center of board, and magnet], instructions on back of box cover, multicolored lithographed board shows fields and flowers and surrounds large metal disk **40.00**

Hurdle Race, boxed board game, ©1905, 16¼ x 11½", 5 pieces [4 round colored wooden counters and spinner], instructions on back of box cover, multicolored lithographed board represents oval track with numerous characters in center and around board **110.00**

"I Don't Know", card game, ca 1903, 5¼ x 4¼", 35 cards and instruction card, box bottom carries advertising for *Pitch-a-Ring Junior* and *Magic Hoops Junior* **15.00**

Jack & Jill, boxed board game, ©1909, 8 x 15½", 5 pieces [4 round colored wooden markers, and spinner], multicolored lithographed board depicts simple track with instructions printed at bottom **50.00**

Jack Straws, skill, ca 1900, 6 x 5", many colored wooded sticks of many shapes and 2 hooks **15.00**

Jolly Tumblers, boxed board game, ca 1895, 22 x 9½", 4 aluminum cylinders each filled with a steel ball, and tan target board, instructions on back of box cover, wooden box partitioned 1¾" wide to hold pieces **95.00**

Junior Combination Board, boxed board game, ©1905, 17 x 8¾", 55 pieces [board folds in half, spinner, 20 checkers, 32 wooden counters, instruction booklet], board multicolored and lithographed on both sides, 12 assorted games can be played **50.00**

Little Boy Blue, boxed board game, ca 1905-10, 12¼ x 12¼", 4 wooden counters and spinner, lithographed board pasted on box bottom with instructions printed on face, track game **50.00**

Little Jack Horner, boxed board game, ca 1910, 8 x 15½", 5 pieces [4 round colored wooden markers and spinner], multicolored lithographed board shows pie in center with instructions printed at bottom, track game **50.00**

Little Orphan Annie Game, 1927, 17 x 8³ x 1½", No. 4359, drawn by Harold Gray **135.00**

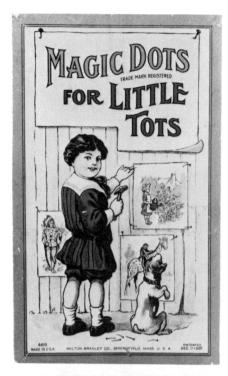

Magic Dots For Little Tots, art, ©1907, 6 x 9⅝″, 12 pieces [10 black and white perforated cards, 2 boxes of tiny cardboard dots to fill in the perforations to create colored picture **30.00**

Magic Squares and Mosaic Tablets, educational, 1869, 7 x 5″, numerous lettered and numbered cardboard squares to instruct and amuse with instruction booklet, inventor is Edward W. Gilman **40.00**

Merry-Go-Round, ca 1910, 6¾ x 5½ x 1″, No. 4688, ... **25.00**

Motor Cycle Game, boxed board game, ©1905, 9″ square, 5 pieces [4 round colored wooden counters and spinner] instructions on back of box cover multicolored lithographed board depicts trail through mountains and around lakes **55.00**

Movable Shadowgraphs, skill, ca 1905, 8½ x 9½″, 5 multicolored lithographed cards showing hands in different positions to create shadow pictures, all have one movable hand **175.00**

Movie-Land Lotto, bingo game, ©1920's, 9½ x 8¼ x 1⅝", No. 4243 . . .**40.00**

Movie-Land Puzzle **55.00**

Moving Picture Game, The, ca 1922, 15 x 9", 5 pieces [4 round colored wooden markers and spinner], multicolored lithographed board represents inside of movie with screen at top, and seats which are really the track, inventor was Howard Garis who wrote the Uncle Wiggily stories and invented the *Uncle Wiggily Game,* instructions on back of box cover **60.00**

North Pole Game, The, boxed board game, ©1907, 13 x 20", 6 pieces [2 dice cups, 2 dice, 2 wooden counters], instructions on back of box board multicolored, lithographed scenes of Arctic, track game **450.00**

Old Maid, card game, ca 1905, 5½ x 6¾", 21 multicolored, lithographed cards, including *Old Maid* . . .**15.00**

Old Maid, card game, ca 1910, 4⅞ x 3⅞",
38 cards and "Old Maid" ... **10.00**

Outboard Motor Race, The ... **40.00**

Peter Coddles,
St. Nicholas Series **15.00**
Peter Coddle's Trip, card game, ca 1925,
6⅛ x 7½", No. 4380, numerous printed
cards and 16 page reading booklet,
booklet is titled "Peter Coddle's Visit to
New York" **15.00**

Peter Coddle's Trip, card game, ca
1905, 6⅛ x 7⅛", numerous printed
slips and reading booklet titled "An
Account of Peter Coddle's Visit to New
York" **15.00**
Peter Coddle's Trip to New York,
card game, ca 1925, 5½ x 6³",
numerous printed cards and reading
booklet **10.00**

Peter Rabbit, boxed board game, ca 1910, 11¼ x 16¼", 3 pieces [2 round colored wooden counters, and spinner], multicolored lithographed board shows Peter Rabbit along path in different predicaments, instructions printed at foot of board **85.00**

Phoebe Snow, boxed board game, ca 1902, 8¾ x 16⅞", 6 pieces [4 colored wooden counters, spinner, and folded board], multicolored lithographed board opens to 16¼" square, pictures Chicago, New York, Rocky Mountains, and San Francisco in each corner and locomotive and cars across center, track game **225.00**

Pigs in the Clover, puzzle, ca 1930, 8" square, 4 steel balls, instructions on back of box cover, board is green and yellow maze **50.00**

Pirate and Traveler, separate board and pieces box, ©1911, 27 x 16¼" board, folds in half, matching 7¼ x 3" box of pieces [metal spinner, 2 counters, 55 cards and instruction sheet], board shows multicolored lithographed map of world **60.00**

Race for The North Pole, boxed board game, ca 1902 5⅛" square, spinner and 2 round wooden counters, solid yellow board with track of black numbers **8.00**

Races, boxed board game, ca 1880;, 4⁷⁄₈ x 3¾", 4 pieces [paper race course, teetotum, 2 cardboard horses on wooden supporters], instructions on face of cover, box is paper hinged . . . **20.00**

Radio Game, boxed board game, ca 1926, 14 x 8", 5 pieces [4 wooden counters and spinner], multicolored lithographed board pasted on inside box bottom, track game **75.00**

Radio Game,
15 x 9 x 1¼", No. 4625 . . . . . **75.00**

Raggedy Ann's Magic Pebble Game, ©1940 and 1941 by Johnny Gruelle Co., 15½ x 8¹¹⁄₁₆ x 1¾", gameboard 16½ x 13", No. 4865, 18 pieces [8 colored bases (2 each of 4 colors), supporting cardboard figures, 1 die, playing board], instructions printed on inside of lid, inside box labelled as *Game of Raggedy Ann, Raggedy Andy and the Wishing Pebble, track* **60.00**

Ring My Nose, skill, ca 1926-28, 8¼ x 12¼", 8 cardboard rings and metal screw for clown's nose, multicolored lithographed board shows same picture of clown as on cover, target game **45.00**

Santa Claus Game, boxed board game, ca 1920-24, 12 x 8½", 5 pieces [4 wooden counters and spinner], multicolored lithographed board pasted to bottom of box, show serveral stockings hung in front of blazing fireplace, instructions printed on face of board **240.00**

Santa Claus Puzzle Box, puzzle, ca 1924-26, 13 x 9", 3 puzzle pictures in black and white on back of box cover, contains 3 multicolored lithographed puzzles each with Christmas theme **200.00**

Scavenger Hunt, 1933, $7^3/_8$ x $5^5/_8$ x 1¼", No. 4239, numerous cardboard tokens representing objects, cards with collecting list, complete with instruction booklet **20.00**

Sectional Animals, puzzle, ca 1900, 11¼" square, multicolored lithographed straight puzzle pieces which form pictures of animals **45.00**

Smitty Game, ca 1930's, 16½ x 8½ x ¾", No. 4254, drawn by Bernd, licensed by Famous Artist Syndicate **110.00**

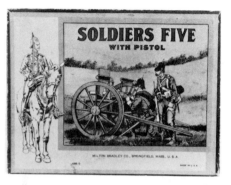

Soldiers Five with Pistol, skill, ca 1915 $10^5/_8$ x 8¼", 10 multicolored lithographed cardboard soldiers on wooden supports, metal and wooden gun, several wooden 'bullets", instructions on back of box cover .. **125.00**

Snap, card game, ©1905, 5 x $7^3/_8$", 32 multicolored lithographed cards instructions on back of box cover **15.00**

Speed Boat Race, track game, ca 1930's, 14¼ x 8¼ x $1^3/_{16}$", No. 4506, box bottom is board **45.00**

Snap, ©1905, 6¾ x 5½", 32 multicolored lithographed cards, instructions on back of box cover **15.00**

Spin It, skill, ca 1910, 7½ x 11", 2 wooden tops and red and gray target board with instructions printed on bottom **18.00**

Spin It, skill, ca 1926, 11 x 7½", 2 wooden tops and red and gray target board with instructions printed on bottom **30.00**

Spinette, skill, ca 1924, 6¾" square, spinner and 10 beads, orange target board with numbered holes, instructions on back of box cover . . . **15.00**

Spoof, card game, ©1918, 7½ x 5½", 61 pieces [52 cards, 8 wooden knobbed sticks and instruction booklet], card backs are orange and white, faces are lithographed orange and black Indian designs **20.00**

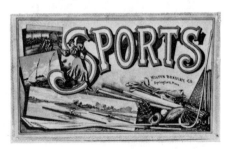

Sports, boxed board game, ca 1910, 15 x 9", 3 pieces [2 round colored wooden counters and spinner], multicolored lithographed board with various sport implements around border, track game **75.00**

Three Little Kittens, The, boxed board game, ca 1910, 7½" square, 5 pieces [4 round colored wooden counters and spinner], multicolored lithographed board with simple track and instructions printed at bottom **35.00**

Stencils, art, ca 1900, 4¾ x 6¾", many tan stencils and sheets of tracing paper **15.00**

Table Croquet, skill, ca 1890, 12½ x 6½", 27 pieces [2 wooden goal posts, 4 table clamps, cloth tape, 4 wooden mallets, 4 wooden balls, 11 wickets, instruction sheet], Wooden box with slide top **75.00**

Three Men in a Tub, skill, ca 1935-36, 11¾ x 8¾", 10 pieces [3 multicolored cardboard figures, wash tub, 2 wooden supports, 3 colored wooden balls, advertising card], instructions on back of box cover **35.00**

3 Men On A Horse, boxed board game, 1936, 19¾ x 10¾ x 1½", No. 4637, based on picture by Warner Bros. Pictures, Int., track game **35.00**

Through The Locks To The Golden Gate, boxed board game, ca 1905, 9 x 15", 3 pieces [2 round colored wooden pieces and spinner], multicolored lithographed board shows Isthmus of Panama, Instructions printed on face of board **85.00**

Tiddledy Ring Game, skill, ©1905, 21¾ x 4½", 8 pieces [4 bone rings, 4 bone winks], multicolored lithographed board pictures pig in center, circle of felt on left side, and target with pins on right side **55.00**

Tiddledy Winks, skill, ca 1905, 6¼" square, 25 pieces [glass cup, 2 green felts, and 20 colored bone winks] instructions on back of box cover **15.00**

Tiddledy Winks, skill, ca 1920's, 7 x 7 x 1½", No. 4218 . . . . **12.00**

Tip Top Fish Pond, skill, ca 1930's 10 x 9 x 1³/₈", No. 4159, 9 pieces [game cardboard, 6 fish, 2 poles with string and hook], instructions printed on game cardboard, stepped game cardboard, multicolored and shaped fish **20.00**

Toddle Top: A Spinning Number Game, ©1939, 9 x 9 x 1¼", No. 4597 . . . . **15.00**

Toonerville Trolley Game, boxed board game, 1927, 17x 8¾ x 1½", No. 4838, based on cartoon characters of Fontaine Fox, track game **120.00**

Tourist, The, A Railroad Game, boxed board game, ca 1900, 15 x 9", instructions on back of box cover, 5 pieces [4 round wooden colored counters and spinner], multicolored lithographed board has picture of old-time locomotive in center, track game **125.00**

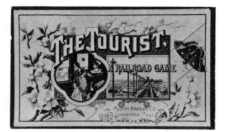

Town Hall, 1939, 12¼ x 8½ x 2", No. 4602, numerous cardboard tokens fit together in domino style to form path, instruction book **20.00**

Toy Town Bank, educational, ©1910, 16 x 10½", 4+ pieces [lithographed teller window like one on cover, 3 supports for window, toy money, account books, checks and deposit slips], instructions on back of box cover, game to teach child rudiments of banking **175.00**

Toy Town Conductors Game, educational, ©1910, 13¾ x 8¾", 5+ pieces [conductor mask, multicolored lithographed folding ticket office, punch, wooden whistle, many tickets, telegrams, passenger checks, etc.], instructions on back of box cover **210.00**

Traps And Bunkers—A Game Of Golf, skill, ca 1930, 9⅛ x 17¾ x 1¼", No. 4091, maneuver clay marbles into holes in board **110.00**

Trips of Japhet Jenkens & Sam Slick, card game, ca 1871, 4¾ x 3¾", numerous printed cards and reading booklet, Bottom of box advertises the game, *Halma* **30.00**

Turn Over, boxed board game, ©1908, 11⅝ x 5", 2 aluminum cylinders each, filled with a steel ball and green target board, box has 1½" partition to hold pieces **35.00**

Two Game Combination, Messenger Boy and Checkers, boxed board game, 8¾ x 17", 30 pieces [4 colored wooden men, spinner, 24 red and black checkers, lift out, folded board], instructions on back of box cover, multicolored lithographed board opens to 16¼" square, with pictures of ticker tapes in each corner, directions printed at bottom between picture of jail and applicants office, track game, reverse side is checker board **75.00**

Two Game Combination, U.S. Mail and Checkers boxed board game, ca 1920, 17 x 8¾ x 1½", No. 4904 .. **145.00**

Vox Pop, 1938, 11¾ x 7⅜ x 1¼", No. 4121, based on "Vox Poppers" radio show of Parks Johnson and Wallace Butterworth, instruction book **20.00**

Walt & Skeezix Gasoline Alley Game, ca 1920, 19¼ x 10 x 1⅝", No. 4516 . . . . **120.00**

War of Nations, boxed board game, ca 1915, 16¼ x 11¼", 11 pieces [10 round wooden counters of 2 colors and spinner], multicolored lithographed board shows map of France and Germany with instructions printed in lower left corner, World War I strategy game **60.00**

Whoopee, ©1929, 5⅜ x 4 x 1",
No. 4314 . . . . **20.00**

Wild Flowers, card game, ca 1900, 4¾
x 3¾", 18 multicolored lithographed
flower cards and 2 blanks, instructions
on face of cover **10.00**

Wyhoo!, ©1897, rules read "©1906",
9¼ x 5", 110 lithographed black and
white cards, instructions on back of
box cover **25.00**

Yacht Race, boxed board game, ca 1905,
8 x 14⅛", 5 pieces [4 round colored
wooden markers and spinner], instructions on back of box cover, multicolored lithographed board shows
water scene with numerous ships and
sailboats, track game **55.00**

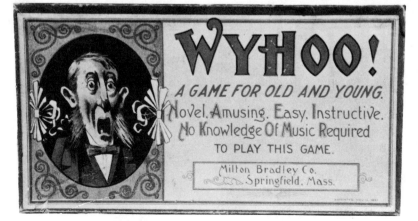

Anagrams, classic, ca 1910, 6¾ x 5½", numerous cardboard letters and instruction sheet **10.00**

Andy Gump, His Game, #4711 • 1924, licensed by Sidney Smith Corp., 4⅛ x ⅜ x 2⅝", #4711, 6 special wooden cubes, numerous cardboard coins, score sheets, dice cup (illustrated), 9 page instruction booklet, strategy dice game **95.00**

Authors, card game, ca 1890, 4¾ x 3¾", 21 cards, lithographed portraits of famous authors, instructions on back of box cover **5.00**

Auto Game, The, boxed board game, ca 1906, 11⅛" square, 5 pieces [4 round, colored, wooden counters and spinner], instructions on back of box cover, multicolored lithographed track shows track through green landscape with various obstacles **240.00**

Cabin Boy, boxed board game ca 1910, 11⅛" square, 5 pieces [4 colored wooden counters and spinner], instructions on back of box cover, multicolored lithographed board has pictures of ship's captain, ship's prison and cabin boy on left side, remainder of board is track **45.00**

Checkered Game of Life, The, boxed board game, ca 1860, 4⅞ x 3⅞" **45.00**

Checkered Game of Life, The, boxed board game, ca 1884, 4¾ x 3¾", box of pieces contains 4 colored wooden markers, 4 cardboard teetotums and instruction sheet; these pieces accompany board of *Checkered Game of Life* **40.00**

Crow Cards, 12 Great Games in 1, card game, ca 1910, 5½ x 4", 52 cards and instruction sheet **15.00**

Down and Out, skill, ca 1928-30, 9½ x 7½", 5 pieces [red metal ringed tower and 4 steel balls] instructions on back of box .cover, target board, has numbered depressions for balls, and two holes to insert tower **25.00**

Drawing Teacher, art, ca 1905, 9⅝ x 6⅞", numerous tan stencils and sheets of tracing paper, instructions on back of box cover **30.00**

Duck On The Rock, skill, No. 4136, 8⅛ x 14⅛ x 1", wooden ball is rolled into holes for points . . . . · **20.00**

Fibber McGee and the Wistful Vista Mystery, The Merry Game of, ©1940, No. 4768 . . . . **28.00**

Fortune Teller, The, ca 1905, 7¼" x 9¼", 2 pieces [multicolored lithographed fortune teller on easel, with wand, with revolving wheel of cards, and instruction sheet **95.00**

Fortune Telling Cards, card game, ©1908, 5⅛ x 6⅝", 33 multicolored lithographed cards, instructions on back of box cover **20.00**

Game of Bamboozle, boxed board game, ©1872, 14¼ x 13¼", 5 pieces (spinner and 4 wooden colored counters], instructions on back of box cover, board is multicolored lithographed map of "The Enchanted Isle", track game **110.00**

Game of Beauty and the Beast, boxed board game, ©1905, 9" square, 5 pieces [4 round colored wooden counters and spinner], instructions on back of box cover, multicolored lithographed board depicts track through forest with wild animals **40.00**

Game of Costumes and Fashions, card game, ©1881, 3⅞ x 5¼", 72 multicolored lithographed cards and instruction sheet **35.00**

Game of Days, card game, ca 1905, 6 x 5", 105 printed cards of important dates of history, instructions on back of box cover **15.00**

Game of Funny Conversation cards, card game, ©1906, 7½ x 5½", 48 cards with red and white backs, instructions on back of box cover **15.00**

Game of Get Busy, card game, ©1906, 7½ x 5½", 48 lithographed cards in black and white, instructions on back of box cover **20.00**

Game of The Lost Heir, card game, ca 1920, 7½ x 6¼", 32 multicolored lithographed cards and instruction sheet, instructions on back of box cover, based on actual news story of kidnapped boy heir **20.00**

Game of The Nebbs, card game, 5¼ x 3¾ x ¾", No. 4041, licensed by Famous Artists Syndicate, cards feature characters from comic strip **45.00**

Game of Robinson Crusoe, boxed board game, ©1909, 8 x 15½", 5 pieces [4 round colored wooden counters and spinner], multicolored lithographed board showing simple track .. **50.00**

Game of Tiger Tom, boxed board game, ca 1920, 12¼ x 12¼", 5 pieces [spinner and 4 wooden counters], directions printed on multicolored lithographed board showing cat in center, track game **55.00**

Game of Twenty Five, card game, ca 1925, 5½ x 4", 60 cards and instruction sheet, cards have red and white backs, and numbered faces **10.00**

Game of What Next or Divided Answers, educational card game, ca 1910, 5½ x 4", 48 cards, red and white, with mathematical problems **10.00**

Game of Words and Sentences, card game, "copyright secured", ca 1875-80, 4¾ x 3¾", numerous lettered cardboard numbers and instruction sheet, play similar to Anagrams **10.00**

Genuine Steamer Quoits, skill, ca 1924, 13½ x 7¼", 8 pieces [2 wooden bases, 2 wooden 4" poles, 8 rope quoits], instructions on back of box cover **25.00**

Grandma's Game of Riddles, quiz, © but no date, ca 1910, 119 printed cards with conundrums and answer booklet **15.00**

Grandma's Geographical Game, quiz, ca 1910, 6¼ x 8¼", 119 cards and answer booklet **15.00**

Happy Family, The, a game of geography & natural history **25.00**

Hialeah Horse Racing Game, boxed board game, ca 1940, 19½ x 12", 11 pieces [folding multicolored board of race track, dice cup, 3 dice, and 6 metal racehorses of different colors], directions on back of box cover .. **75.00**

Jolly Clown Spinette, skill, ©1932, 9¼ x 9¼ x 1⅛", No. 4012 ...... **40.00**

Magnetic Jack Straws, skill, ©1920, 5½ x 3¾", 5 pieces [3 magnets, 2 metal clowns, numerous metal sticks, some with different colored wooden shapes at one end] instructions on back of box cover **15.00**

Modern Authors, card game, ca 1890, 7⅝ x 5½", 60 cards of illustrated famous authors, instructions on back of box cover **12.00**

Pitch-A-Ring, skill, ca 1905, 11 x 6¼", 12 pieces [wooden base, center post, 4 corner posts, 3 large cardboard rings, 3 small cardboard rings], target game **35.00**

Poetical Pot Pie or Aunt Hulda's Courtship, educational, 1868, 4⅝ x 3⅛ x ¾", approx. 120 strips with quotes by famous authors, 16 pages, 2⅞ x 4½" instruction book containing story with blanks, instructions contain advertisements for other games, inside of box lid is advertisement for *Blown-Up Steamer Puzzle* bottom of box is advertisement for *The Game of Corona or Banner & Crown* **75.00**

Quiz-Me, Game of Geography,1940, 5½ x 6¾ x 1", No. 4777, cards and instruction book **15.00**

Sam Slick From Weathersfield to Paris and the Exposition, card game, ca 1870, ¾ x 4½", numerous printed cards and reading booklet, advertising on back of box cover is *The Blown-Up Steamer,* an early Milton Bradley **45.00**

Saratoga: A Horse Race Game, ca 1920's, 19½ x 11¾ x 1¾", No. 4541 .... **45.00**

Spelka, card game, ca 1908, 7¾ x 5¾", 52 cards and instruction booklet, card backs are red and white card hands "Spelka", faces are green and white and lettered **12.00**

Tall Structures, card game, ca 1905, 5 x 6", 35 cards and instruction card, blue backs and lithographed in black and white on faces showing world's famous tall buildings, advertising for games, national standards, and *Game of Transportation* on bottom of box .. **30.00**

Three Guardsmen, The, separate board and pieces box, 18½ x 18½", board folds in half, 6¼ x 3³/₅", matching box of playing pieces, 53 wooden counters, directions on back of box cover, multicolored board Fox & Geese board showing Three Musketeers in each corner **65.00**

Two Game Combination, Steeple Chase and Checkers, boxed board game, ca 1910, 17 x 8¾", 30 pieces [4 round colored wooden counters, spinner, 24 red and black checkers and lift out, folded board], instructions on back of box cover, multicolored lithographed board opens to 16¼" square and pictures race track, reverse side is checker board **50.00**

"Uncle Wiggily" Game, separate board and pieces box, ca 1918, 16 x 16", multicolored lithographed board folds in half, matching box of playing pieces 6 x 5¼", contains 4 colored wooden counters, 105 white cards and 35 red cards **30.00**

What Do You Know About Fine Arts, card game 1939, 8½ x 5½ x 1¼" **20.00**

BUEHL BOOK CO.

Atlanta, GA   ca 1900

Wiggs, card game, ©1903, 3¾ x 2¾", 65 cards and instruction sheet, cards have red and white backs with pictures of Mrs. Wiggs and cabbages, L.T. Hodges, inventor, based on Mrs. Wiggs and the Cabbage Patch **25.00**

CADACO-ELLIS

Chicago, IL   ca 1940's

Yankee Doodle, educational ©1940, 9⅝ x 7⅛ x 1⅝", numerous pieces [quote cards, red, white and blue counters, alphabet letters, and "Yankee Doodle" answer book 4⅜ x 5¼", 8 pages], instructions on inside of lid . . . **25.00**

CARDBOARD PRODUCTS CO.

"Ole" Thousand Faces,   ca 1920's
ca 1925 . . . . **20.00**

N. D. CASS CO.

Athol, MA   ca 1920's

Bowling Alley, skill, 1920-22, 21 x 4¾", 12 pieces [10 wooden ten pins, 2 wooden balls], bottom made of wood with triangle of black spots for pin positions **35.00**

67

H. B. CHAFFEE MANUFACTURING CO.

New York, NY   ca 1870's

Parcheesi, board game [see Selchow & Righter] **50.00**

Flinch, card game, ca 1875, 5½ x 3¾", 151 pieces [150 black and white numbered cards and instruction sheet] **10.00**

CHAFFEE & SELCHOW

New York, NY   ca 1890's

Dewey at Manila, card game, Starry Flag Series, 1899, 6½ x 5", 53 pieces [52 cards, instruction booklet], cards pink and white backs showing Dewey and ship *Olympia* **40.00**

Game of Old Mother Goose, boxed board game, ca 1890, 8 x 16", 5 pieces [4 wooden counters and spinner], directions on back of box cover, multi-colored board printed on cardboard box bottom, shows track and pictures of Mother Goose and son Jack . . **125.00**

THE CHICAGO GAME CO.

Chicago, IL   ca 1910's

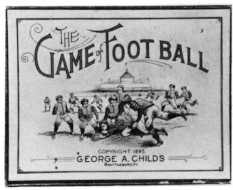

The New World To World Airship
Race **395.00**

Pana Kanal, ©1913 .... **145.00**

GEORGE A. CHILDS

Brattleboro, VT   ca 1890's

Game of Football, The, boxed board
game, 1895, 11¾ x 8¾", 7 pieces
[wooden bench, 4 team cards, board
of football field which folds in
half, card with instructions and spinner affixed] **175.00**

CINCINNATI GAME CO.

Cincinnati, OH

ca 1890's-1910's

Successors to The Fireside Game Company, Cincinnati, Ohio.

A Trip Through Our National Parks: Game of Yellowstone, card game, ca 1910, 6⅝ x 5⅛ x 1", No. 1122, each card with different scene of park **30.00**

Flags, card game, ©1896, 2⅞ x 3¾", No. 1111, 52 cards plus "Crown" card, directions pasted on back of cover **30.00**

Fractions, educational card game, ©1902, 2¾ x 3¾", 56 cards and instruction booklet **20.00**

Game of Flowers, educational card game, ©1899, 2¾ × 3¾", No. 1126, 52 cards, directions on back . . **25.00**

Game of Words, educational card game, ©1903, 2⅝ × 3⅝", 113 numbered and lettered cards and instruction booklet **25.00**

Game of Words, card game, 1903, 111 cards plus 20 page instruction book, cards are black on white, 1¾ x 2½", box is black on red, 2⅝ x 3¾" . . **20.00**

Illustrated Mythology, card game ©1901, 2¾ x 3¾", No. 1129, 50 cards, backs have statue of Juno, directions pasted on back of cover **25.00**

In Castle Land, The Cincinnati Game Co. ©1896, 2¾ x 3¾", No. 1113, 52 cards, directions pasted on back of cover **25.00**

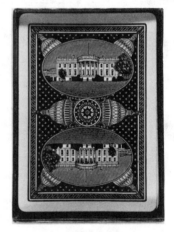

In The White House, educational card game, ©1896, 2¾ x 3¾", No. 1115, cards have White House in blue and white on backs, faces depict each president with his accomplishments, 44 cards, instructions pasted on back of cover **25.00**

Mayflower, The, card game, ©1897, 2¾ x 3¾", No. 1121, 53 cards [52 and 1 advertising card] instruction booklet pasted on back of box cover . **25.00**

Our National Life, educational card game, ©1903, 2¾ x 3¾", 52 cards and instruction booklet, game teaches American history **25.00**

C. M. CLARK PUBLISHING CO., INC.

Boston, MA ca 1900

Stage, card game ©1904, 7½ x 2¾", 68 pieces [66 cards, 1 advertising card, instruction sheet], cards picture famous opera stars and entertainers of the day—Lillian Russell, Eva Tanguay, Tony Pastor, Edwin Booth, etc. ... **65.00**

E. O. CLARK

New York, NY ca 1890's

Charge, The, boxed board game, Tokalon Series, ca 1899, 19³/₈ x 10¼", No. 354, 26 pieces [2 kings, 24 soldiers], instructions on back of cover, game board on box bottom, lithographed multicolored, fox and geese format, Rough Riders charging Spanish fort, game is response to Spanish-American War **140.00**

Hippodrome, The, boxed board game, Tokalon Series, ca 1900, 19½ x 10¼", 6 pieces [3 tiddledys, 3 winks], instructions on back of cover, game board printed directly on cardboard box bottom, black ink, tiddledy-wink format, 7 animal heads at top with scores and 3 penalty figures **60.00**

Owl and The Pussy Cat, The, boxed board game, Tokalon Series, ca 1905, 19¼ × 10½", No. 351, 5 pieces [4 wooden counters and cardboard spinner], instructions on back of box cover, multicolored board lithographed on box bottom, pictures sea with turkey and pig on isle in center, board sides are wood **150.00**

CLARK & SOWDON

New York, NY   ca 1890's

Authors Illustrated, card game, Tokalon Series ©1893, 6⅜ x 4½", 74 pieces [72 cards, instruction sheet and advertising card], cards have black and white pictures of authors **15.00**

Game of Golf, The, boxed board game, Tokalon Series, ca 1905, 19 x 10½", No. 352, 5 pieces [4 wooden counters and cardboard spinner], instructions on back of cover, multicolored lithographed board on box bottom, picturing golf course, board sides are wood **225.00**

Game of Rough Riders, The, boxed board game, Tokalon Series, ca 1900, 10¼ x 19¼", No. 353, 5 pieces [spinner, 4 wooden counters], instructions on back of cover, multicolored lithographed board with Rough Riders, Indians, Buffalo, etc., track game **120.00**

Game of Wang, The, Tokalon Series, 1892, 6½ x 4½ x 1", ... **30.00**

Hunting The Rabbit, boxed board game, Tokalon Series, ca 1890-95, 15 x 7½", 6 pieces [spinner, 4 counters and board], directions on back of cover, multicolored lithographed board lifts out, shows track with hunter, rabbit and 2 dogs **55.00**

Tete-a-Tete and Lucko, boxed board game, ©1892 by E.W. Hall, box 7¼ × 6⅛ × 1⅝", gameboard 5¾ × 6¾", 24 pieces [20 playing pieces, gameboard, two dice, wooden cup], instruction sheet printed one side, 5 × 8", board has blue ground, white dots, 4 color groups of 5 pieces, strategy **50.00**

CLEMENT TOY CO.

North Weare, NH   ca 1920's

Hexagons, puzzle, 1924, 18 moveable wooden puzzle parts in large oak frame, instruction sheet **50.00**

Yacht Race, boxed board game, Tokalon Series, ca 1890–95, 15 × 7½", 5 pieces [4 cardboard yachts in wooden stands and spinner], directions on back, multicolored lithographed track pasted on bottom **55.00**

Game of Old Maid, The, card game, Tokalon Series, ©1892, 6 × 4¼", 32 pieces [31 multicolored cards and instruction sheet] **20.00**

L. J. COLBY & CO.

Chicago, IL ca 1890's

Literature Game, card game, ©1897 by A. W. Mumford, 3¾ x 2½ x 1³⁄₈" **10.00**

A Game of Characters, American, educational card game, ©1889, 2½ x 3½", 100 cards, inventors were F. G. Decker and O. F. Decker **15.00**

DAVID C. COOK PUBLISHING CO.

Elgin, IL ca 1900

Bible Game of New Testament Books, card game, ca 1900, 3 x 4¼", 38 cards and instruction sheet **10.00**

COOKSON & SULLIVAN

San Francisco, CA ca 1920's

Pe-Ling, classic, ©1923, 16 x 4½", 280 pieces [144 cardboard tiles, 4 wind buttons, 2 dice, 4 tile racks, 4 blank pieces, 120 counters and 2 instruction booklets, Mah Jongg type game .. **30.00**

CHARLES M. CRANDALL

Montrose, PA; Waverly, NY 1830-1929

Crandall made building blocks, croquet sets and acrobats, and was the first to apply the tongue and groove principle to blocks and figures. The company is best known for District Schoolhouse figures. Beginning in 1867, Crandall supplied building blocks to E. G. Selchow. In 1889 Selchow & Righter Company became sole agents for Crandall's *Pigs In Clover* game.

Crandall's Building Blocks, Diamond Edition blocks, 1867, 4¾" square, grooved, wooden lettered pieces in wooden, dovetailed box, dated 1867 .... **225.00**

WM. CROSBY

Boston, MA   ca 1840's

Game of The Races, The, framed, 1844, frame 24 x 18", game 18 x 14½", oval track, lithographed and hand painted, lithographer Bouve and Sharp, Boston, game would have closed like a book and buckled, game pieces, teetotum and ivory markers would be kept in pouch of buckle **1250.00**

CUTLER & SALEEBY CO., INC.

Springfield, MA   ca 1900-20's

India Bombay, boxed board game, ca 1920-25, 11 x 10", 18 pieces [16 wooden counters, 2 dice], bottom partitioned into 1 x 10" compartment for playing pieces and 10 x 10" multicolored lithographed board, directions printed on face of board, different animals pictured on each side, *Parcheesi* - type track **30.00**

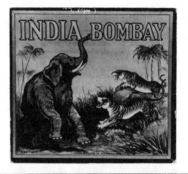

Ski-Hi: New York to Paris, #2117, ca 1927, 12³/₄ x 7³/₄", 5 pieces, die and 4 metal planes, multicolored lithographed board showing ocean, NYC and Eiffel Tower. Track game . . **85.00**

O. F. & F. G. DECKER

Buffalo, NY   ca 1880's

In addition to the games listed here, the Deckers invented *A Game of Characters, American* which was manufactured by L. J. Colby & Corp. of Chicago, Illinois, copyrighted 1889.

A Game of Characters, Foreign, educational card game, ©1889, 2½ x 3½", 100 cards **15.00**

A Game of Cities, educational card game, ©1889, 2½ x 3½", 100 cards **15.00**

A Game of the States, educational card game, ©1887, 2¾ x 3⁵/₈", 50 cards **15.00**

A Game of The World, educational card game, ©1889, 2¾ x 3½", 100 cards **15.00**

DE LUXE GAME CORP.

ca 1920's

Flip It: Auto Race and Transcontinental Tour, ca 1920's, 11³⁄₈ x 9³⁄₈ x 1", 4 pieces [2 metal cars, inside gameboard, die], lid serves as second game board, instruction sheet (typed) **45.00**

GEORGE B. DOAN & CO.

Chicago, IL
ca 1900

Worth While, card game, 1904, 4⁵⁄₈ x 2⁵⁄₈", 69+ pieces [68 cards, instruction sheet and numerous round counters], backs of cards are gray and white, showing marble edifice overlooking lagoon **15.00**

CARL F. DOERR

ca 1910's

New York, NY; Yonkers, NY

"Cat", boxed board game, ca 1915, 10½ x 5½", board and 2 clay marbles, directions on back of cover, simple baseball game **25.00**

DOREMUS-SCHOEN CO., INC.

Brooklyn, NY
ca 1930's

Classic Derby, boxed board game, ca 1930-35, 14½ x 9¼", 113 pieces [deck or poker cards, box of 100 poker chips, race track board, 6 recording boards with wooden supports, 4 derby racers and instruction sheet] **50.00**

WALLIE DORR CO.

New York, NY
ca 1920's

Foolish Questions, card game, 1924-26, 5½ x 3¾", 55 pieces [52 black and white illustrated cards, scorecard, advertisement, instruction sheet], illustrations are by cartoonist Rube L. Goldberg **20.00**

Touring, card game, 1926, 5¼ x 3¼", 100 cards and instruction sheet, card backs are red and white picturing old touring car; Wallie Dorr was inventor of this game, which Parker Brothers later bought **25.00**

R. L. DOW & CO.

Hartford, CT

ca 1890's

Number 10 Puzzle, The, puzzle, 1897, 5⅛" square, 10 pieces [5 round wooden red markers and 5 round wooden black markers, all numbered], instructions pasted on back of cover, bottom of box has red and yellow numbered, lithographed circle **15.00**

SARAH H. DUDLEY

Berlin, MA

ca 1910's

Our Bird Friends, card game, ca 1910, 52 cards and instruction sheet **15.00**

G. H. DUNSTON

Buffalo, NY

ca 1900

Botany, card game, ca 1903-05, 8 x 5½", 52 multicolored lithographed cards of flowers, directions on back of cover **25.00**

DURABLE TOY & NOVELTY CORP.
(Radio Questionaire Corp.)

New York, NY   ca 1920's

Radio Questionaire, Radio Questionaire Corp., quiz, ©1928, 9½ x 9½", 6 pieces [6 quiz cards], box bottom has raised black cardboard with attached metal indicator and light bulb, battery operated **40.00**

E. C. EASTMAN

Concord, NH   ca 1860's

Commanders Of Our Forces, card game, 1863, 4½ x 3½", 80 cards and instruction sheet, cards, printed in black and white, name famous battles and generals of the Civil War **75.00**

EDUCATIONAL CARD & GAME CORPORATION

New York, NY   ca 1920's

Bild-A-Word, educational card game, 1929, 6¼ x 6¼ x 1" **15.00**

ELTEN GAME CORPORATION

New York, NY   ca 1930's

Balance The Budget, card game, ©1938,
5½ x 3¾", 57 pieces [52 cards, 4 score
sheets, instruction sheet], cards multicolored, with black backs showing red
dollar sign **20.00**

THE EMBOSSING COMPANY

Albany, NY   1870-1957

    The company was established by J. W. Hyatt, Jr. It had a tremendous production
of dominoes, checkers and blocks. The company was bought out by Halsam Products
in 1957.

Bottoms Up, checker game, ©1934, 6¾
x 3 x ⅝", embossed pig on bottom of
checkers **25.00**
Flapper Fortunes, ©1929, 3⅝ x 2½ x
1¹¹⁄₂₈" **15.00**
Frisko,©1937, 10⅞ x 8 x 2¼", No. 701,
71 pieces [32 tiles with numbers 1 to 6,
3 die, die cup, 34 chips, knock on wood

chips], instructions on inside of box lid,
blocks are in 4 colors, numbered 1 to
6 for each color **25.00**
Checker Alphabets, educational, ca
1890, 5¼ x 2¼", 24 round red and
black wooden checkers with numbers
and letters **25.00**

J. M. FARMER

ca 1930's

Farmer Electric Maps, ©1938 by J. M. Farmer, 18³/₁₆ x 11 x 1¹³/₁₆", 6 stiff board maps, 16³/₈ x 10³/₈", "D" shape on left to correspond to contact track **45.00**

THE FIRESIDE GAME CO.

Cincinnati, OH

ca 1890's

In The White House, card game, ©1896, 2¾ x 3¾", 44 cards with Capitol building on backs, instruction booklet stickered to back of box cover, political game **25.00**

Maple Grove, card game, ©1896, 2⁵/₇ x 3⁵/₇", No. 1105, 53 cards, directions on back of cover **20.00**

Chestnut Burrs, ©1896, 2¾ x 3¾ x ⁷/₈", No. 1106 . . . . **20.00**

Game of Artists, card game, ©1897, 2¾ x3¾", No. 1117, 52 cards, instructions on back of cover **25.00**

Game of Dixie Land, card game, ©1897, 2⁵/₈ x 3⁵/₈", No. 1118, 54 pieces [52 cards, instruction card, advertising card] **25.00**

Game of Strange People card game, ©1895, 2⁵/₈ x 3⁵/₈", No. 1100, 52 cards and advertising card, directions pasted on back of box cover **25.00**

White Squadron, card game, ©1896, 2⁵/₈ x 3⁵/₈", No. 1108, 52 cards and advertising cards, picturing ships of the U.S. Navy, directions pasted on back of cover **35.00**

A. FLANAGAN COMPANY

Chicago, IL 　 ca 1880's-1910's

Geography Game, ca 1910's, 5¾ x 4¹/₁₆ x 1¹/₁₆", 100 cards, 2¼ x 3⁵/₁₆", 5 questions per card; by Harriet B. Rogers **20.00**

Helps To History, or Historical Games With Cards, 1885, 4¹/₈ x 3⁵/₈ x 1"; by D. Eckley Hunter **20.00**

Mother Earth's Produce Game, by Mrs. C. B. Sheldon, 4¾ x 3", 58 black and tan lithograph cards, instruction booklet **20.00**

FLINCH CARD CO.

Kalamazoo, MI

Parker Brothers bought the company in 1936.

Bourse, card game, ©1903, 3⅝ × 5⅛", 80 cards and instruction card, backs are red and white fleur de lis . . . **20.00**
Flinch, card game, ca 1904, 3¾ × 2", 150 cards, title card and instruction booklet **10.00**

Roodles, card game, ca 1912, 5½ × 3¾", 58 pieces [56 cards, trademark card, instruction sheet]; invented by A.J. Patterson, cards have swastika design **20.00**

C. S. FRANCIS & CO

New York, NY

Multiplication Merrily Matched, educational card game, ca 1850, 142 cards, hand painted **120.00**

H. M. FRANCIS

New Game of Aesop, framed, 1861, 28½×23", multicolored lithographed board, and hand painted . . . **950.00**

WILLIAM FULD

Baltimore, MD

--OUIJA--
Pronounced WE-JA
Trade Mark Registered in United States and Canada
Egyptian Luck Board
MADE BY
WILLIAM FULD
Baltimore, Md. - - U. S. A.
Patented in United States and Canada.

Ouija, 1920, 6⅛ × 4¼ × ⅞", Fuld bought rights from Elijah Bond in
1892 and later sold them to Parker Brothers **15.00**

83

FULLER, UPHAM & CO

Providence, RI   ca 1870's

Pinafore, card game, 1879, 55 cards and instruction booklet, cards show silhouetted nautical figures, backs have picture of cat-o'nine tails **40.00**

FULTON SPECIALTY CO.

Elizabeth, NJ   ca 1920's

Wizard, The, quiz, ©1921, 8⁷/₁₆ x 8³/₈ x 1¼", 3 pieces [cardboard insert, directional arrow, question disk], directions printed in center circle of cardboard insert, question and answer ... **35.00**

SAML. GABRIEL SONS & COMPANY

New York, NY   ca 1930's

Game of Black Sambo, boxed board game, ca 1939, 17¼ x 13", No. T264, pieces include several round cardboard pancakes, 4 cardboard tigers and 1 Sambo, 5 wooden brackets, spinner, instruction sheet, and folding board, board is multicolored, lithographed and 14¾ x 19" when open . . **275.00**

Crusade, 14½" square **25.00**

W. W. GAVITT PRINTING AND PUBLISHING CO.

Topeka, KS   ca 1900

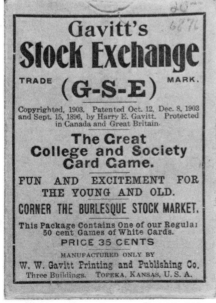

Gavitt's Stock Exchange, ©1903, 3½ x 2½ x ¾" **10.00**

Gavitt's Stock Exchange, ©1904 . . . . **10.00**

THE GEM PUBLISHING CO.

Game of Treasure Island, separate board and pieces box, ©1922-23, board folds out to 16½" square, matching pieces box is 4 x 2½", 13 pieces [2 dice cups, 2 wooden dice, 8 colored wooden counters, instruction sheet], board has lithograph of pirate and treasure on front signed "C. H. Trotter" and has pictures of pirates, cannibals, islands, and in the center an inn **55.00**

GIBSON GAME CO.

Boston, MA

ca 1910's

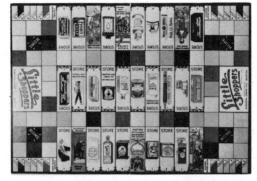

Little Shoppers, 1915,
14½ x 11¾" **240.00**

A. C. GILBERT

New Haven, CT

ca 1910's

Meteor Game, skill, 1916, 7½ x 5", 64 pieces [1 metal board with 61 holes, 1 metal forceps, 61 multicolored clay marbles, instruction booklet], instruction booklet lists manufacturer as F. Ad. Richter & Co., No. 1 game . . . **20.00**

GLOW PRODUCTS CO.

New York, NY

ca 1920's

Ticker, boxed board game, 1929, 16 x 2½", 146 pieces [cloth board, 2 dice, dice cup, 14 stock certificates, 7 composition markers, 16 cards, 104 clay chips, instruction sheet], within box is black cylinder, with green, yellow, and red trading cloth board wrapped around it, inside cylinder is black box containing dice, markers, cards and chips, top of cylinder becomes dice cup **75.00**

GOODENOUGH & WOGLUM CO.

New York, NY   ca 1930's

Game of Bible Lotto, The, ca 1930's, 7³/₈ x 5³/₈ x 1" 8.00

E. J. GOODRICH

Oberlin, OH   ca 1900

Game of Forty-Two, card game, ca 1900, 2½ x 3½", cards that look like   dominoes 10.00

J. JAY GOULD

Boston, MA   ca 1870's

Who Do You Love Best, card game, 1876, 7½ x 5", 76 pieces [70 cards with let-   ters on them, 4 wooden pegs, 2 pencils], directions on cover 25.00

GREBNELLE NOVELTY CO.

Philadelphia, PA   ca 1910's

Championship Base Ball Parlor Game, boxed board game, ©1914, 22 x 9¼", 30 pieces [envelope containing 2 dice and 20 yellow and blue players' position disks, photograph of 1914 Boston Braves, booklet listing names of players   for all 16 leagues and 120 clubs, instruction booklet, 3 score cards and folding board which opens to 18 x 22"], board shows multicolored base ball diamond; Henry Ellenberg, Jr., is inventor 1550.00

CARL W. GRIMM

Musical Casino card game, 1927, 2¾ x 3¾", 49 cards and instruction sheet, cards show major and minor

ca 1920's

chords of the scale; Grimm was inventor **30.00**

KERK GUILD

Utica, NY

ca 1930's

A. A. Milne's Winnie—The—Pooh Game, ©1931, by Stephen Slesinger, Inc., 10½ x 16 x ¾", 5 pieces [cloth playing surface, 19¾ x 19", 4 metal Pooh bears, spinner], track . . **110.00**

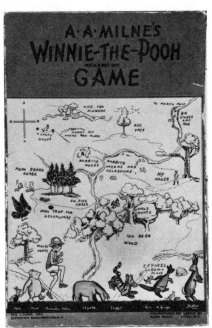

PAUL K. GUILLOW

Wakefield, MA   ca 1920's

Crash, separate board and pieces box, 1928, 14½ x 13¾", 15 pieces [board multicolored track, 12 metal planes, directions sheet, spinner], directions list NuCraft Toys, Wakefield, Massachusetts; Guillow, inventor of game, also invented *Lindy*, now owned by Parker Brothers **55.00**

THE HAMILTON-MYERS CO., PUBLISHERS

Middletown, PA

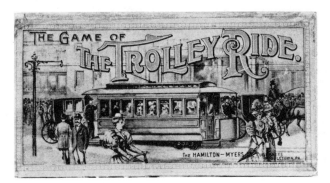

Game of The Trolley Ride, The . . **65.00**

S. L. HILL

Williamsburgh, NY   ca 1870's

Hill's Spelling Blocks, Blocks, 1872, 6"
square, No. 4A, wooden box with slide
cover, contains 16 wooden blocks lithographed with pictures and letters, first
patent issued in 1858 . . . . . . **375.00**

S. L. HILL & SON

Brooklyn, NY   ca 1870's

Kindergarten Building Blocks, blocks,
ca 1875, 8¼ × 5¾", No. 13,
wooden box with slide cover of old
Santa Claus, 28 colored wooden
blocks, lithographed with pictures
and letters **400.00**

HOME GAME CO.

Chicago, IL   ca 1900's

Bunco, card game, 1904, 5½ x 3⅞   **Game of Five Hundred,**
x 1" . . . . **10.00**   card game **10.00**

C. I. HOOD CO.

Lowell, MA   ca 1890's

Hood's War Game, card game, ca 1898, 2¾ x 3¾", 52 cards and instruction card, game deals with Spanish-American War, but is also advertising game, with red, white & blue, American flag and Hood logo on card backs **40.00**

E. I. HORSMAN

New York, NY   ca 1880-1918

Primarily jobbers in games and novelties, the company now manufactures dolls.

Halma, separate board and pieces box, ©1885, pat May 29, 1888, 5½ x 4", box has 40 pieces [folding 15¾" square board, 38 wooden counters, instruction booklet], board has green and light green squares 19 x 19, with gold dotted corners; this game was forerunner of Chinese checkers, inventor was G. H. Monks **40.00**

Magnetic Jack Straws, skill, ©1891, 5½ x 3½", 39 pieces [35 metal "straws" of different shapes, metal forceps, pronged magnet, metal clown and horseman figures], instructions pasted on back of cover **20.00**

J. W. HOSFORD & CO.

                                                                    ca 1880's

Game of The United States and Territories, card game, ca 1885, 2¼ x 3¾", 50 cards and instruction card, played like *Authors* **15.00**

I. B. & W. CO.   ca 1880's

Tiddledy Winks, 8⅜ x 4⅛ x 1⅞" wooden box with sliding lid **35.00**

Tiddledy Winks, 5½ x 4 x 1¾", wooden box with sliding lid **30.00**

IDEAL BOOK BUILDERS

Chicago, IL   ca 1910's

Jolly Faces Game, The, puzzle, 1912, 7¾ x 8¼", 21 pieces [4 card board multi-colored faces, paper packet with 16 puzzle pieces of mouths, eyes and noses] **35.00**

INTERSTATE SCHOOL SERVICE

New York, NY   ca 1920's

American History in Pictures, educational, set of 4, 1926, 4¾ x 3¾", each set has 15 black and white cards **20.00**

D. P. IVES & CO.

Boston, MA   ca 1840's

Guessing Game, card game, ca 1843-45, 3⅝ x 2⅜", 28 cards, all hand painted, Rebus-type game **140.00**

H. P. IVES

Salem, MA   ca 1840's

Game of Dr. Busby, card game, ca 1844, 3 x 4⅜", 20 cards hand painted, instruction sheet on box bottom **140.00**

W. & S. B. IVES

Salem, MA   1830-1884

The Ives Brothers were in the book publishing, binding and selling business at the Old Corner Bookstore. They supposedly manufactured the first U. S. board game, *Mansion of Happiness*. George S. Parker purchased the rights to the Ives games shortly after the death of Stephen Ives.

French Puzzle Brain, puzzle, 1851, $4^3/_8$ x $2^3/_8$", 18 wooden (mahogany) puzzle pieces **55.00**

Game of Dr. Busby, card game, ca 1845, 2½ x 3¾", 20 cards, all hand painted **125.00**

Mansion of Happiness, framed, 1843, frame 24 x 18", game 18 x 14½", oval track, lithographed and hand painted, lithographer S. W. Chandler & Bros., Boston, game would have closed like a book and buckled, game pieces, (teetotum and ivory markers) would be kept in pouch of buckle . . . **1000.00**

Master Rodbury and His Pupils, card game, 1844, $2^5/_8$ x 3¾", 18 cards and one instruction card, all cards hand painted, game invented by Anne Abbot **160.00**

MOTHER BUSBY, Dr. Busby's Wife

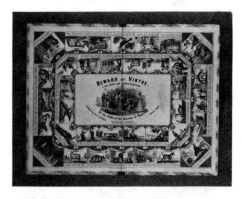

Reward of Virtue, framed, 1850, 23½ x 20", lithographed by J. H. Bufford & Co., Boston, hand-painted, invented by Anne Abbot **1500.00**

Characteristics, card game, 1843, 3¼ x $2^3/_8$", 52 pieces [50 cards, 1 key card and instruction card], invented "by a lady" believed to be Anne Abbot, who devised *Mansion of Happiness* . . . **150.00**

Flags of The Nations, card game, ca 1844, 2½ x $3^3/_8$", 40 cards, all hand painted, of world flags, U.S. flag has 30 stars in it **110.00**

JAY MAR SPECIALTY

ca 1940's

What's My Name?, ca 1940, 15¼ x 10¼ x 1⅞", based on radio program by Edward Byron and Joe A. Cross **35.00**

J. W. KELLER

ca 1890's

Hounds and Hares, card game, 1894, 2½ x 3½", 51 cards [40 cards for game, instruction card, 10 cards of players' testimonials for game], backs of cards same as cover on box **15.00**

KNAPP ELECTRIC, INC.
(Division of P. R. Mallory)

New York, NY; Port Chester, NY   1894-1929

David W. Knapp, inventor, made tool sets and wood working kits in addition to battery operated games. The company was first known as "Knapp Electric and Novelty Co."

Ges-it Game **40.00**
Knapp Electric Questioner, 13⅝ x 9⅜ x 2⅛" **45.00**

Pyramids, ca 1930's 6 x 6 x 1" . **15.00**
The Tell Bell, 1928, 13⅞ x 9½ x 2⅛" **30.00**

LEE AND SHEPARD

Boston, MA   ca 1840's

Old Pampheeze And His Comical Friends, card game, ca 1840, 3¼ x 4¼", 25 pieces [24 cards and instruction sheet], 12 cards red and white, 12 cards black and white, look like pasteboards, game played like *Happy Families* **75.00**

LEONARD MFG. CO.

Grand Rapids, MI   ca 1910's

Snook, card game, ca 1910, 3³/₈ x 1³/₈", 28 cards and instruction sheet, pink backs, played like dominoes **25.00**

OSWALD B. LORD

New York, NY   ca 1930's

Politics Game, The, separate board and pieces box, ©1935, pieces box 8½ x 2½", 35 pieces+ [30 speech cards, 3 dice, large quantity pins, $6,000,000 in currency, score card pad, instruction sheet], board 29 x 17" open, shows map of U.S. signed T. Miller, Oswald B. Lord is inventor of game and Lord sold his game to Parker Brothers . . **45.00**

LUBBERS & BELL MFG. CO.

Clinton, IA   ca 1920's

Blox-O, boxed board game, ©1923, 6¾ x 6⁵/₈ x 1³/₁₆", 23 pieces [gameboard, 22 pegs 7+4 red, 7+4 green], instructions pasted on inside of box lid, strategy **10.00**

Puzzle-Peg, boxed board game, ca 1920, 6¾ x 6¹¹/₁₆ x 1³/₁₆", 33 pieces [gameboard, 32 green wooden pegs], instructions printed on inside of box lid, circular gameboard with red and white blocks, strategy **15.00**
Toss-O, 1924 6¾ x 6¾ x 1¹/₈" . . . **7.50**

THE MADMAR QUALITY COMPANY

Utica, NY ca 1900

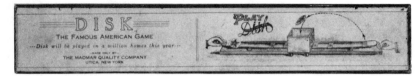

Disk, ca 1900, 20⅜ x 3½ x 2⅝″, 15 pieces [playing piece, 12 disks, 2 snappers], no instructions, long board with center container, springing (launching) stick to each side, base painted red, box green, 6 green and 6 red, 1¹¹/₁₆″ cardboard disks with points **40.00**

CHARLES MAGNUS

ca 1850's

New National Snake Game, framed, ca 1855, 27¾ x 23½″, multicolored lithographed and hand-painted, board game folds in half **1550.00**

MAH-JONGG SALES COMPANY OF AMERICA

San Francisco, CA ca 1920's

Mah-Jongg, Classic, ©1923, 16 x 3½″, 143 pieces [136 cardboard tiles, 4 wooden tile racks, 1 teetotum, 1 direction sheet for spinner, 1 instruction booklet], rules by J. P. Babcock, ©1920 . . . . **25.00**

MARKS BROTHERS CO.

Boston, MA ca 1930's

Horse Race Game, separate board and pieces box, ca 1930-33, pieces box 14 x 3½″, 14+ pieces [6 metal horses, 4 wooden traces, 3 dice, instruction sheet and large quantity of silver cardboard coins], folding board opens to 47 x 17¼″ race track, multicolored, lithographed, labeled "Belmont Park" **225.00**

MILTON BRADLEY

PLATE 1

PLATE 2

PARKER BROTHERS

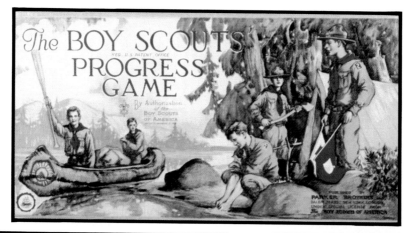

PLATE 3

OTHER GAME COMPANIES

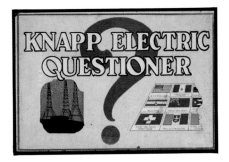

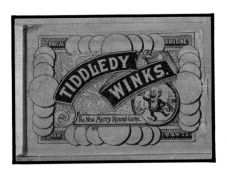

PLATE 4

OTHER GAME COMPANIES

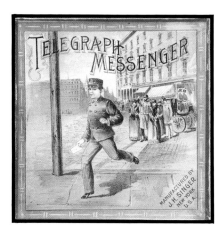

PLATE 5

CARTOON THEME GAMES

PLATE 6

SPORTS GAMES

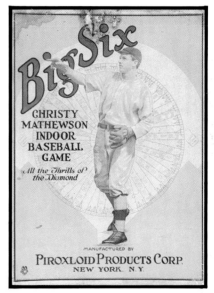

PLATE 7

TRANSPORTATION GAMES

PLATE 8

THE MARTIN CO.

North Adams, MA   ca 1900-10's

Home Games, game assortment ca 1900-05, 12½ x 10", 83 pieces [2 paper balloons, 15 round wooden lettered disks, 14 wooden colored sticks, metal cup, tape with 2 supports, wooden dice cup with 6 wooden lettered dice, wooden cup, 2 wooden and cardboard paddles, 16 celluloid winks, 4 metal disks, 2 bubble blowers, 4 cardboard rings, 4 wooden pegs, envelope containing 7 instruction sheets for 7 different games.] **140.00**

Flitters, skill, ©1899, 6 x 9", 7+ pieces [wooden striker, wooden button, 4 wooden dowels and quantity of multi-colored tissue paper disks, called flitters] **35.00**

Young Magician's Outfit, skill, ca
1905-10, 8½ x 7", 9 pieces [wand, ball,
sticks and string, cup with marble, tape,
2 sticks, instructions] **95.00**

MARX, HESS & LEE, INC.

ca 1930's

Four Dare Devils, The, ©1933, 20³/₁₆ x
9½ x 1¾", gameboard with four
baseball figures with extended arm

holding cup upright, bell, four marbles,
instruction sheet 6¾ x 9³/₈ . . **65.00**

MASON & PARKER MFG. CO.

Winchendon, MA   ca 1920's

Ten-Pins, skill, ca 1920 9¾ x 5¼", 13
pieces [10 wooden pins and 3 red,
wooden balls], cover states "By C. E.

Bradley Corporation, Brattleboro,
Vermont" **25.00**

MAYHEW & BAKER

Boston, MA   ca 1850's

Game of The Young Peddlers, card
game, 1859, 6¼ x 4¼", 37 pieces [16
cardboard strips, 2 peddler cards, 18
money cards, instruction sheet], cards

are hand colored; this company also
published *Gipsey Fortune Teller, The
Game of the School in an Uproar,* and
The Game of Yankee Land . . . **140.00**

ELIZABETH M. MCDOWELL AND FREDERICK MELLOR

ca 1910's

Allie-Patriot Game, card game, ©1917, 2⅝ x 3⅝", 48 cards and instruction booklet, backs picture blue Statue of Liberty, game deals with World War I, distributed by *E. I. Horsman* . **40.00**

MCDOWELL MFG. CO.

Pittsburgh, PA

ca 1930's

Aeroplane Race, No. 60 "Mac" Whirling, ca 1930's, 10¼ x 10¼ x1¾" **75.00**

MCGILL & DELANY

ca 1880's

 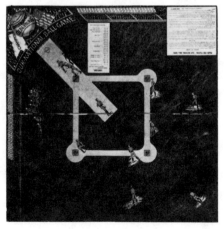

Our National Ball Game, separate board and pieces box, ©1886, folding board opens to 17½ x 17½", showing multicolored lithograph of baseball diamond and printed directions, played with 2 dice, behind home plate is printed "Loag The Printer" and the initials E.I.H. in a diamond; could be Horsman, and McGill and Delang are inventors **650.00**

McLOUGHLIN BROTHERS

New York, NY   1828-1920

Although company was created in 1828, games were not manufactured until the 1850's. The company was sold to Milton Bradley in 1920.

McLoughlin Brothers relocated several times. These addresses should help collectors with dating the company's games, as the games are not dated in every instance. Locations and dates are as follows; all addresses are located in New York, NY:

Tryon Road (1828-35); 24 Beekman Street (1835-61); 30 Beekman Street (1861-70); 71-73 Duane Street (1870-86); 623 Broadway (1886-92); 874 Broadway (1892-98); 890 Broadway (1898-1920).

Aesop's Fables, (Aunt Louisa's Cube Puzzles), blocks, ca 1888, wooden box 9¾ x 1½", 5 multicolored lithographed pictures and 30 multi-colored lithographed 6-sided blocks to create those pictures plus the one on the cover **350.00**

Air Ship Game , The, Yankee Doodle Series, boxed board game,©1904, 12½ x 12½ x ¾", 6 pieces [spinner, 4 colored pieces, game board pasted to base], instructions printed on inside of lid, track **375.00**

Air Ship Game, The, Standard Series, boxed board game, 1912, shows ©1904, 12¼ x 12¼", 5 pieces [spinner, and 4 colored wooden counters], instructions on back of box cover, board shows water scene with balloon in center, track game **375.00**

Boys Own Football Game . . . 550.00

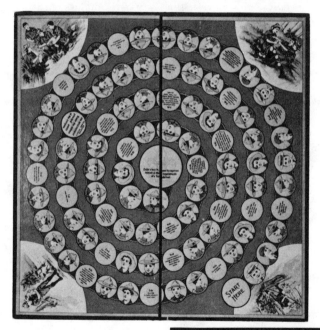

Boy Scouts, separate board and pieces box; ca 1910's, gameboard 18¹¹/₁₆ x 18¾", pieces box 6¼ x 4⅛ x ⅞", 7 pieces [spinner, 6 colored checkers], instructions [lost, but noted on label of pieces box], round track gameboard with 90 stops, multicolored, profiles of scouts plus scout rank requirements, wood playing pieces **225.00**

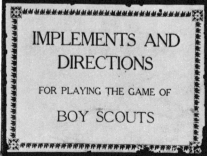

IMPLEMENTS AND
DIRECTIONS

FOR PLAYING THE GAME OF

BOY SCOUTS

Chiromagica, mechanical game, ca 1870, 11½″ square wooden box with slide cover, directions on center disk pasted to glass top inside box, mechanical hand pointer beneath glass revolves in circle to answer ques- tions, besides answer sheet No. 1 (pink) pasted on glass, answer sheets No. 2 and No. 3 included, together with 3 matching question disks to set in center, answers are magnetically cued to questions **650.00**

Cinderella Or Hunt The Slipper, card game, ©1887, 4½ x 6¼″, 43 cards and instruction sheet, cards are multicolored lithographed illustrations of various objects, played like *Old Maid* **30.00**

Cut Up Animals Spelling Slips, puzzle, ca 1900, 9 x 12″, black and white pictures of animals that puzzle slips make on back of box cover, puzzle slips are multicolored and lithographed **120.00**

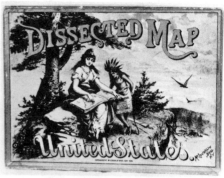

Derby Steeple Chase, The, boxed board game, ©1890, 10¾ x 10¼", 23 pieces [4 wooden counters, 18 wooden chips and spinner], instructions on back of box cover, multicolored lithographed board of race track opens up to 19½ x 10", oval picture in center shows horses leaping over obstacle **75.00**

Dissected Map of The United States, puzzle, ©1887, 9¼ x 6¾", several multicolored lithographed interlocking puzzle pieces and paper map of U.S. **45.00**

Diamond Game, The, boxed board game, ca 1885, 4 x 8¼", instructions on back of box bottom, spinner result numbers on back of box cover, multicolored lithographed board pictures diamond with affixed spinner, and 6 pegs, baseball game **75.00**

Errand Boy or Failure and Success, The, boxed board game, ©1891, 14½ x 15", 5 pieces [4 colored wooden counters, cardboard spinner], instructions on back of box cover, multicolored lithographed board pasted to inside box bottom, errand boy pictured in center, prison and application office in each corner, checker board-type track game, Horatio Alger theme **550.00**

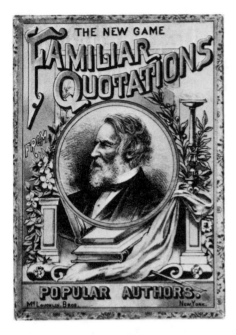

Familiar Quotations card game, ca 1890, 3¼ x 4¼", 42 cards with pink backs and instruction card, no illustrations 20.00

Farmer Jones' Pigs, boxed board game, ca 1885, 8½ x 14½", Popular Series No. 406, 6 wooden counters and spinner, multicolored lithographed board shows pigs in cornfield in center, with numbered squares around perimeter, track game 120.00

Flag Game, The, card game, ©1887, 8½ x 4½", 137 pieces [60 flag cards, 16 tickets and instruction booklet], cards depict flags of different nations, multicolored lithographed, wooden box, inventor is M. M. Babbitt, Massachusetts 50.00

Game of Bagatelle, boxed board game, ©1898, 7¾ x 15½", instructions on back of box cover, 11 wooden counters, multicolored lithographed board is checkered with domino layout on one side, track game **120.00**

Game of Bang, Pearl Series, boxed board game, ©1903, 7¾ x 15½", No. 5160, 7 pieces [6 round wooden counters and spinner], instructions on back of box cover, multicolored lithographed board **140.00**

Game of Base-Ball, boxed board game, ©1886, 17⅛ x 9½", 21 pieces [9 lead fielders, 8 colored wooden markers, 2 spinners (detached metal arrows) board, and instruction booklet], multi- colored lithographed board of baseball diamond shows 2 spinners for fielders and batters, in which spinner pieces fit, wooden box **2500.00**

Game of Bicycle Race, boxed board game, ©1891, 10¼ x 19½", 11 pieces [4 wooden counters, 6 colored numbered wheel men, spinner], instructions on back of box cover, multicolored lithographed board on box bottom shows bicyclers in center, wooden box, track game . . . **795.00**

Game of Catching Mice, gem series, boxed board game, ©1888, 7¾ x 15½", 15 pieces [2 men, 12 round, wooden counters and spinner], instructions on back of box cover **175.00**

Game of Bicycle Race, boxed board game, ©1895, 21¼ x 12½", 6 pieces [4 lead bicycles and 2 spinners], instructions on back of cover, multicolored lithographed board represents map of countryside and towns, wooden box, track game **900.00**

Game of City Life or The Boys of New York, card game, 1889, 5 x 6½", 44 multicolored lithographed cards and instruction booklet **25.00**

Game of District Messenger Boy, The,
American Boy Series, boxed board
game, 1899, 19½ x 10½", 5 pieces
[spinner and 4 wooden counters], instructions on back of box cover, multicolored lithographed board pasted on
bottom of box, track game . . **225.00**

**Game of Familiar Quotations From
Popular Authors,** card game, ca 1888, 4
x 5", 55 cards, not illustrated . **20.00**

Game of Dr. Fusby MD.card game ca
1890, 4½ x 6¼", instructions on back
of box cover, 48 multicolored lithographed cards divided into 12 sets,
played like *Happy Families* . . **30.00**

Game of Fish Pond, The, skill, 1890, 19½
x 10¼", 26 pieces [2 wooden fish poles,
24 numbered cardboard fish], instructions on back of box cover, board sets
into box bottom, leaving 1¼" wide partition to hold poles and fish, multicolored lithographed board pictures
pond with pond lilies and frogs and has
numerous slits in which to stand fish,
wooden box **125.00**

Game of Flags, card game, ©1896, 5½ x 7½", instructions on back of box cover, 54 multicolored lithographed flag cards and 72 printed disks **75.00**

Game of Hunting, The New, boxed board game, ©1904, 16½" square, 20 pieces [4 colored lead dogs, spinner and arrow, 14 round lithographed "game" pieces], instructions on back of box cover, multicolored lithographed board depicts country terrain with brook and mountain, contains slots to insert game pieces, center has opening to insert spinner and arrow, wooden box **1100.00**

Game of Golf, boxed board game, ©1896, 13½ x 15½", 23 pieces [4 wooden playing pieces, 18 round wooden counters and spinner], instructions on back of box cover, multicolored lithographed board depicts golf course, train, wagon and golf players, board lifts up at top to reveal 4" wide partition for gaming pieces, wooden box **975.00**

Game of Just Like Me, card game, ©1899, 4¼ x 5¼", instruction sheet is ©1888, 30 multicolored lithographed cards **40.00**

Game of Leap Frog, boxed board game, ca 1890, 8½ x 10¼", 17 pieces [8 round red wooden counters, 8 round yellow wooden counters, cardboard spinner], instructions on back of box cover, multicolored lithographed board pasted on inside box bottom shows frogs, pond, pond lilies, etc., track game **115.00**

Game of Old King Cole, card game, ©1888, 3½ x 4¾", 32 multicolored lithographed cards and instruction sheet **35.00**

Game of Mail, Express Or Accommoda-tion, boxed board game, ©1895, 22½ x 15", 45 pieces [4 lead trains, 2 dice cups, 4 dice, 35 cards], instructions on back of box cover, multicolored litho-graphed board depicts map of U.S., Bradley and Poates, Engravers, New York, wooden box **1800.00**

Game of Phoebe Snow, boxed board game, ©1899, 8½ x 16¼", 6 pieces [4 colored wooden counters, spinner and board], multicolored lithographed board opens to 16¼ x 15¾", shows train labled "Phoebe Snow" traveling through center and city scenes and Rocky Mountain scene in each corner, track game **300.00**

Game of Playing Department Store, boxed board game, 1898, 22½ x 15", instructions on back of box cover, 54 counters, numerous round cards representing money, and indicator, board multicolored lithographed, attached to box bottom, shows all manner of merchandise for sale, spinner hole for indicator in center, wooden box **1400.00**

Game of Puss in The Corner, The, card game, ©1888, 3½ x 4⁷⁄₈", 32 multicolored lithographed cards and instruction sheet, cards illustrated with cats, mice and rats **40.00**

Game of Pussy and The Three Mice,
boxed board game, ©1890, 10½ x
10¾", 5 pieces [large wooden counters
representing cat, 3 smaller wooden
counters representing mice, and
2 arrow spinner], instructions on
back of box cover, multicolored lithographed board opens to 10¼ x 19¾",
pictures cats and mice in center and
smaller pictures around sides, track
game **225.00**

**Game of Round The World With Nellie
Bly,** boxed board game, ©1890, by J. A.
Crozier, 12¼ x 12¼", 5 pieces [4
wooden counters, spinner], instructions on back of box cover, multicolored lithographed board is circular
track of Nellie's Trip, © inside is 1904,
wooden box **240.00**

Game of Shoot The Hat, Punch and Judy
Series, card game, ©1892, 4¼ x 3¼",
instructions on back of box cover, 21
multicolored lithographed cards with
blue backs **35.00**

Game of Snip, Snap, Snorum, Banner
Series, card game, ca 1898, 3⅞ x 4⅞″,
48 multicolored lithographed cards,
numerous cardboard counters and instruction sheet, cards numbered and illustrated with face caricatures, "Pooling" game **25.00**

Game of The Christmas Jewel, Pearl
Series, boxed board game, ©1899, 7¾
x 15½″, 4 pieces [2 wooden round
counters, wooden piece representing
"Jewel" and spinner], instructions on
back of box cover, multicolored lithographed checker-type board with
numbers, track game **175.00**

Game of Strategy, boxed board game,
©1891, 19¾ x 10½″, 33 pieces [16
white checkers, 16 black checkers,
and spinner with 2 arrows], directions
on back of box cover, multicolored
lithographed board shows cavalry
headquarters in center, and implements of war in each corner, back-
gammon-type design around sides,
strategy game **240.00**

Game of The Telegraph Boy, boxed board game, ©1888, 17$\frac{1}{8}$ x 9½", 4 lead messenger boys, metal arrow and board which folds in half, multicolored lithographed board has instructions printed at bottom, and in right corner is spinner and hole for arrow, scenes of training school, applicants' office and prison in other three corners, wooden box, track game to reach goal of "President," Horatio Alger-type theme **310.00**

Game of The District Messenger Boy, or Merit Rewarded, boxed board game, ©1886, 9$\frac{3}{8}$ x 17$\frac{1}{8}$", 4 lead messenger boys folding board opens to 17 x 16¼", and is multicolored and lithographed with prison, training school and applicants office in each corner, plus affixed spinner in lower right corner, directions printed on bottom of board, wooden box track game, Horatio Alger theme **250.00**

Game of The Man in The Moon, boxed board game, ©1901, 14½ x 15", instructions on back of box cover, 24 round wooden counters, multicolored lithographed checker board picturing moon's phases, wooden box, strategy game **4500.00**

Game of The Telegraph Boy, boxed board game, ©1888, 18¾ x 17", 4 lead messenger boys and spinner arrow, multicolored lithographed board is part of box bottom with 1¼" wide partition to hold game pieces, instructions printed on bottom of board and spinner to No. 4 is in one corner with hole for arrow, other corners of board show training school, prison, applicants' office, wooden box, board is track game with "President" as goal, Horatio Alger theme **1900.00**

Game Of To The North Pole By Airship, boxed board game, 1897, 19½ x 10¼", 5 pieces [spinner and 4 colored wooden counters], multicolored lithographed board depicts map and ships, track game **850.00**

Game Of The Visit Of Santa Claus, boxed board game, ©1899, 14¼ x 15", No. 605, 38 pieces [36 cards, spinner, and wooden counter], instructions on back of box cover, multicolored lithographed board has center picturing Santa Claus and other scenes of Santa in his work shop around the sides, track game **2500.00**

Game of Tobogganing At Christmas, boxed board game, ©1899, 19½ x 17", 4 lead Santas driving sleigh with 1 reindeer and spinner, board is actual bottom of game with lift up hinge, beneath which game pieces are held, multicolored lithographed board shows children on toboggans and staircases, track game resembling *Chutes and Ladders*, wood box **1750.00**

Game of Toll Gate, A, boxed board game, ca 1890, 15½ x 13½", 20 pieces [2 dice, 2 dice cups, 16 wooden counters], instructions on back of box cover, multicolored lithographed board is part of box bottom with 1½" wide partition at side to hold game pieces, wooden box, track game **450.00**

Game of Trip Round The World, boxed board game, ©1897, 22½ x 16", 14 pieces [4 dice cups, 4 dice, 6 lead yacht pieces], instructions on back of box cover, multicolored lithographed board depicts globe map, 3³/₈" w. flap lifts up to reveal gaming pieces, wooden box **1500.00**

Game of Topsy Turvey, The, boxed board game, ©1899, 15 x 14½", 26 pieces [4 wooden men, 4 smaller men, 17 round wooden counters and spinner], instructions on back of box cover, multicolored lithographed board, *Parcheesi* type, wooden box, track game **500.00**

Game of Wide Awake, The, boxed board game, ©1899, 15¼ x 14½", 25 pieces [spinner and 24 wooden counters], instructions on back of box cover, board on wooden box bottom, multicolored, lithographed track format, center picture shows western figures with guns and horses and the label "battle ground", 4 smaller scenes on each side **475.00**

Games of John Gilpin, Rainbow Back-gammon and Bewildered Travelers, separate board and pieces box, ca 1875, wooden board, 9 x 18", looks like book volume and opens to 18" square, multi-colored and lithographed, block spinner, instruction booklet and wooden markers **650.00**

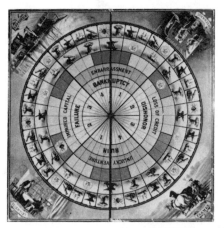

Games Of Monopolist, Mariner's Compass and Ten Up, separate board and pieces box, 1878, numerous pieces [block, 2 arrowed spinner, instruction booklet, colored cardboard money, many round colored wooden counters], triple combination board, when closed, looks like book volume, opens to 18" square, multicolored and lithographed **600.00**

Games Of The Pilgrim's Progress, Going To Sunday School and Tower of Babel, boxed board game, 1875, 9¼ x 18½", 4+ pieces [block, 2 arrowed spinner, 3 instruction booklets, several colored wooden counters], wooden board, multicolored and lithographed on both sides, slips out of slipcase and resembles book volume, opens to 18½" square, all track games **1000.00**

Game of Stars and Stripes Or Red, White and Blue, boxed board game, ©1900, 16½ x 18", 53 pieces [2 dice cups, 2 dice, 44 small silver stars, 1 large star and 4 lead soldiers carrying American flag], instructions on back of box cover, red, white and blue checkered board with field of stars in center, wooden box, track game . . .**2500.00**

Good Old Aunt, The, boxed board game, ©1892, 10½" square, 61 pieces [spinner, 40 white and 20 red counters], instructions on back of box cover, multicolored lithographed board pasted on box bottom is same picture as that on cover, "Pooling" game **175.00**

Grandmama's Improved Arithmetical Game, card game **30.00**

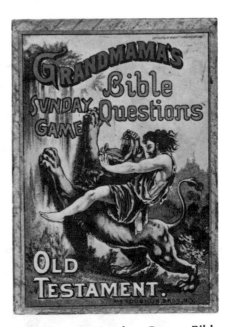

Grandmama's Improved Geographical Game, educational card game, 1887, 6¼ x 4½", 120 numbered printed cards and instruction and answer booklet **30.00**

Grandmama's Sunday Game: Bible Questions, Old Testament.,quiz, ©1887, 4½ x 6¼", 100 question cards, instruction and answer booklet **30.00**

Home Fish Pond, The, skill, ca 1890, 12″ square, instructions on cover, 4 wooden poles, several numbered fish with wooden supports, multicolored lithographed board pasted to box bottom depicts pond with frogs, pond lilies, bird, etc. **110.00**

Home Scroll Puzzle, puzzle, ©1898, 7⅛ x 9¼″, No. 540, multicolored lithographed interlocking puzzle pieces **95.00**

House That Jack Built, The, card game, ©1887, 6¼ x 4½″, 44 multicolored lithographed cards and instruction booklet **30.00**

House That Jack Built, The, card game, ca 1890, 3¼ x 4⅜ x 1⅛″ **25.00**

Jack Straws, skill, ca 1890, 6⅜ x 4⅞″, hook and numerous numbered natural wood pieces of different shapes, wooden box **35.00**

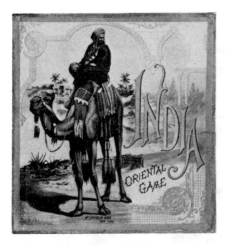

India, An Oriental Game, boxed board game, ca1890-95, 14½ x 15″, instructions on back of box cover, 16 round wooden counters and spinner, multicolored lithographed board with star motif in each corner, wooden box, actually is game of *Parcheesi* .. **110.00**

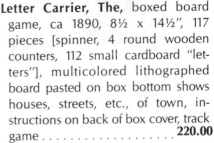

Letter Carrier, The, boxed board game, ca 1890, 8½ x 14½″, 117 pieces [spinner, 4 round wooden counters, 112 small cardboard "letters"], multicolored lithographed board pasted on box bottom shows houses, streets, etc., of town, instructions on back of box cover, track game **220.00**

Lotto, classic, ca 1885, 10½ x 6", numerous pieces [box of glass markers, 24 numbered cards, many round wooden numbers], instructions on back of box cover, wooden box trunk **25.00**

Madame Le Normand's Mystic Cards Of Fortune, card game, ca 1882, 36 black and white illustrated cards and instruction sheet **40.00**

Madam Morrows Fortune Telling Cards, card game, ©1886, 4¼ x 6", 36 red, black and white cards, plain blue backs, and instruction sheet . **30.00**

Merry Game Of Old Bachelor, The, card game, ©1892, 5 x 6½", 48 multicolored lithographed cards and instruction card, played like *Old Maid* **35.00**

New Fox and Geese, The, card game,
ca 1888, 6¼ x 4½", 33 multicolored
lithographed cards and instruction
sheet **30.00**

**Peter Coddle and His First Trip To
New York,** card game, ca 1890, 4¼
× 5¼", numerous small cards with
pink backs and objects printed on
them and instructions and story
booklet **25.00**

Picture Puzzle Steamship, puzzle,
©1896, 19¼ x 7¾", multicolored
lithographed interlocking puzzle
pieces, wooden box **300.00**

Red Riding Hood And The Wolf . . 50.00

Rival Policemen, boxed board game, ©1896, 21×12¼", 23 pieces [2 wooden dice cups, 4 dice, 4 lead policemen, 13 wooden counters (crooks)], instructions on back of box cover, multicolored lithographed board streets of a city, 2½" w. flap of board lifts up to reveal pieces, wooden box, track game . . . **1425.00**

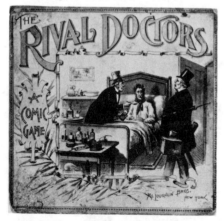

Rival Doctors, The, boxed board game, 1893, 10½ x 10¼", 5 pieces [4 wooden counters and spinner], instructions on back of box cover, track game **110.00**

Robinson Crusoe, boxed board game, ca 1890, 7½" square, instructions on front of box cover, 2 wooden counters and spinner, multicolored lithographed board pasted on box bottom has numbers and pictures of Robinson Crusoe, ships, parrot, etc., track game **35.00**

Round Game Of Tiddledy Winks, skill, 1890, 4⅝ x 3½", 30 pieces [1 wooden cup, 4 large round colored "Tiddledies" of bone, 24 smaller round colored "Winks" of bone, instruction booklet **20.00**

Round The World With Nellie Bly, 1890, © by J. P. Drozier, 8¾ x 16¼ x 1¼", ... **325.00**

Royal Game Of Kings And Queens, The, boxed board game, ©1890 and 1892, 20 x 11½", No. 429, 40 pieces [6 knights and 14 pawns, two sets], instructions on back of cover, game board, 17 x 11¼", centered in bottom creating wells at each end for pieces, multicolored, lithographed, strategy format, light blue and beige blocks, court scenes at corners **125.00**

Scouting Game, No Title, 1914, 16 x 9", 24 pieces [tent, flag, 22 multicolored lithographed scouts standing in wooden supports], tent has "Headquarters" printed on it, flag has 13 stars **325.00**

Skit Scat, card game, ©1905, 6¼ x 4⅝", instruction sheet pasted on back of box cover, 24 numbered multicolored lithographed cards showing cat in various positions around fish bowl .. **25.00**

Snake Game, boxed board game, ca 1888, 7³/₅" square, 5 pieces [4 wooden counters and spinner], instructions on front cover, multicolored lithographed board on box bottom, shows track game on snake **35.00**

Soldier Ten Pins, skill, ca 1890, 8¾ x 7¼", 12 multicolored lithographed soldiers with wooden supports, wooden cannon, and several wooden cannon "bullets" **120.00**

Susceptibles, The, boxed board game, ©1891, 15 x 16", 48 pieces [1 wooden "leader", 4 "companions", 5 colored wooden aids, 8 checker "susceptibles", 6 additional colored companions], instructions on back of box cover, multicolored lithographed board depicts "90's" scenes all around perimeter, center is squares with star in middle, 1½" partition on side holds pieces, wooden box, strategy game . **600.00**

Up The Heights Of San Juan, puzzle, ©1898, by F. D. Maher, 18 x 13½", multicolored lithographed puzzle pieces, depicts battle of Spanish-American War **275.00**

What D'ye Buy, ©1887, 6½" x 4⁷/₈", 85 pieces [12 large "trade" cards, 72 smaller merchandise cards, instruction sheet], cards are multicolored lithographed with gray and white flowered backs. **45.00**

Whirlpool, boxed board game, ca 1899, 7¼" square, No. 408, instructions printed on cover, 12 round, wooden counters and spinner, multicolored, lithographed board shows shipwreck in center and nautical scenes in each corner **25.00**

Young Folks Historical Game, card game, ca 1890, 6¼ x 4½", 36 cards and instruction sheet **25.00**

A New Dissected Map Of The United States, puzzle, ©1887, 12 x 8", puzzle pieces making up map of U.S., wooden box **60.00**

Bo Peep Game, boxed board game, ©1895, 15 x 13½", instructions on back of box cover, 34 wooden pegs, multicolored lithographed board has Little Bo-Peep in each corner, with 17 peg holes on upper and bottom sides, board hexagonal in shape with peg holes, wooden box **175.00**

Box of Pictures To Paint **20.00**

Cock Robin and His Tragical Death, card game, ca 1880, 6¼ x 4½", 42 cards and instruction booklet, backs of cards mottled green and white, faces of 12 are picture cards, others are multicolored lithographed answer cards . . . **30.00**

Color Box, art, ©1897, 10¼ x 11¼", No. 7910, 33 pieces [2 paint trays, 1 paint brush, 5 crayons, 24 picture cards for painting], instructions on back of cover **65.00**

Comical Conversation Cards, card game, 1869, 2⅝ x 2⅛", 36 question and answer cards illustrated in black and white **55.00**

Criss Cross Spelling Slips, Set One, puzzle, ca 1885-88, 8¾ x 10", sliced multicolored lithographed puzzle cards, wooden box, artist's signature at bottom "William Momberger" . . **75.00**

Cut Up Animals Scroll Puzzle, puzzle, ca 1885, 10¾ x 11¼", multicolored lithographed pieces, 2 puzzles, cat lithograph on back of cover, wooden box **150.00**

Cut Up Pictures, puzzle, ca 1885, 10³/₅ x 8½", multicolored lithographed pieces, wooden box **125.00**

Dissected Map Of The United States, puzzle, 1894, 14⅝ x 9½", puzzle pieces make multicolored interlocking lithographed map of U.S. **75.00**

Double Eagle Anagrams, card game, ©1890, 4½ x 6¼", numerous cardboard letters and instruction booklet **20.00**

Elite Conversation Cards, card game, 1887, 3½ x 4¾", 48 question and answer cards and instruction card, not illustrated **10.00**

Game Of Bear Hunt, separate board and pieces box, 1870, 5½ x 9⅛", 20 pieces [16 round wooden counters, 3 piece double teetotum and instruction sheet], board opens like book to "Nine Men's Morris" game on left and target track game on right **110.00**

Game of Bobb, skill, ©1898, dated 1892, 18½" square, 9 pieces [2 brass weighted "bobbs", 4 wooden legs, 2 wooden mallets, and board, which acts as table], instructions on back of box cover, board is multicolored lithographed and dovetailed with metal strips on all sides to hold pegs for scoring, wooden box **750.00**

Game of Comical Snap, card game, ©1903, 4¼ x 5¼", instructions on back of box cover, 24 multicolored lithographed cards **20.00**

Game Of Cousin Peter's Trip To New York, card game, ca 1898, 4¼ x 3¼", 28 cards and instruction sheet . . . **15.00**

Game of Don'ts and Old Maid, The, Banner Series, card game, ca 1905, 5 x 4", 48 multicolored lithographed cards and instruction sheet . . **20.00**

Game Of Familiar Quotations From Popular Authors, card game, ©1887, 3⅞ x 4⅞", 75 cards and instruction sheet, not illustrated **10.00**

Game of Familiar Quotations From Popular Authors, card game, ca 1865, 3¼ x 4⅛", 75 cards and instruction card, cards are not illustrated, played like *Happy Families,* some cards feature Black caricatures **20.00**

Game of Fish Pond, The, Improved,
skill, 1890, 17¼ x 4", instructions on
back of box cover, 3 poles and several
numbered fish, board inserted into box
bottom, multicolored and lithographed represents fish pond with
several slots for fish **110.00**

Game of Guess Again, The, card game,
ca 1890, 5 x 6⁵/₇", No. 4310, 36 multicolored lithographed cards and instruction sheet **30.00**

Game Of Hens and Chickens, card
game, 1875, 7¼ x 4½", 49 multicolored lithographed cards, block spinner with 2 arrows and instruction
booklet, wooden box **120.00**

Game Of Hide and Seek, boxed board
game, ©1895, 23¾ x 15½", instructions
on back of box cover, 4 colored
wooden counters and one for "hat"
multicolored lithographed board has
wooden spinner affixed in center, each
corner has wooden cup inserted with
removable cover and picture of a
dragon, pictures of clowns are on each
side, wooden box, checkerboard track
game **575.00**

Game of Little Jack Horner, The, card
game, ca 1888, 3½ x 4¾", 49 multicolored lithographed cards and instruction cards, cards illustrate different
fruits used in pies **40.00**

Game Of Musical Authors, card game,
1882, 4³/₈ x 5¾", 98 cards and instruction cards, card backs picture a lyre,
wooden box **35.00**

**Game Of Nations Or Quaker Whist,
The,** card game, 1898, 5½ x 4", 52 cards
and instruction sheet, cards multicolored and lithographed with gray
floral backs **30.00**

Game Of Old Maid, The, card game,
©1904, 4⁷/₈ x 3⁷/₈", 41 pieces [40 cards
and instruction sheet] **20.00**

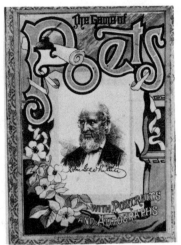

**Game of Poets With Portraits and
Autographs, The,** card game, ©1886,
6 x 8½", 64 cards and instruction sheet,
cards illustrated in black and white,
wooden box **35.00**

Game Of Snap, Punch and Judy Series,
card game, ©1892, 4¹/₈ x 3¹/₈", 20
multicolored lithographed numbered
cards, instructions on back of box
cover **15.00**

Game Of Standard Authors, card game,
ca 1885-90, 6½ x 4½", 56 cards and instruction sheet, cards have red and
white backs, faces are black and white
illustrations of various authors and
printed book titles **10.00**

Game Of The Harlequin, The, boxed
board game, ©1895, 7¾ x 15½", 25
pieces [24 round wooden counters and
spinner], instructions on back of box
cover, board multicolored, lithographed on box bottom, shows picture of
harlequin in center **135.00**

Game of The Spider's Web, boxed board
game, ©1898, 8½ x 10¼", 5 pieces [4
colored wooden counters and spin-
ner], instructions on back of box cover,
multicolored lithographed board
shows web with many spiders, squir-
rels, bird and fox and ducks . . **95.00**

Game Of The Telegraph Messenger Boy, card game, ca 1890's, 24 position cards, numerous transfer cards, 4 page instruction booklet of cardboard **75.00**

Game Of Tight Rope, separate board and pieces box, 1870, 5½ x 9⅛ 20 pieces [16 round wooden counters, 3 piece double teetotum and instruction sheet], board opens like book to "Nine Men's Morris" game on left and target game on right **100.00**

Games Of Go Bang, Tivoli and Fox and Geese, separate board and pieces box, ca 1878, 16 x 8", board multicolored and lithographed opens up like book to 16" square, numerous pieces and instruction booklet **125.00**

Games Of Life's Mishaps & Bobbing 'Round The Circle, The, boxed board game, ©1891, 14½" square, 39 pieces [6 round wooden markers, 2 arrowed spinner, 32 paste board counters], instructions on back of box cover, multicolored lithographed board lifts out and has reverse side for second game, both are track games, instructions state each game ©1888 & 1885 respectively **400.00**

Games Of The Captive Princess Tournament and Pathfinders, boxed board game, 1888, 7½ x 14½", 13 pieces [board, 4 wooden counters, 6 round card board knights, spinner, instruction sheet], board is multicolored and lithographed on both sides, folds in half, one side shows princess in castle and knight fighting dragon, other side shows two tracks **110.00**

Grandmama's Game Of Riddles, card game, ca 1865-70, 5 x 3¾", 124 numbered and printed black and white cards and yellow answer booklet, conundrum game; company's address on cover is 24 Beekman St., New York City, an early address **45.00**

Grandmama's Improved Arithmetical Game, card game, ©1887, 4½ x 6¼", 119 numbered printed cards and instruction and answer booklet, not illustrated **25.00**

Home Scroll Puzzle, puzzle, ©1897, 7¼ x 9¼", multicolored lithographed interlocking pieces **95.00**

Junior Combination Board, separate board and pieces box, ©1905, 16" square, matching pieces box 12 x 3" with checkers, balls and bowling pins, carom rings and instruction booklet board, multicolored and lithographed on both sides **55.00**

Little Santa Claus A•B•C Blocks, ca 1890, 5" square, 16 multicolored lithographed blocks **120.00**

Logomachy, card game, ©1874 by F. A. Wright, 8⅞ x 4½", 70 multicolored lithographed alphabet cards, instructions on back of cover **55.00**

Logomachy Or War Of Words, ©1889, box 6⅜ x 4⅞ x 1¼", cards depict letters of alphabet, some have nice illustrations **30.00**

Lotto, classic, ca 1888, 6⅜ x 3⅝", 12 green and tan cards, numerous wooden square numbers and cardboard covers, instructions spell game "Loto" instructions on back of box bottom **20.00**

Lotto, classic, ca 1905, 8 x 5 3/8", No. 325, 24 green and white numbered cards, numerous round wooden numbers, many square glass markers, instructions on back of box cover . . **20.00**

"Messenger", The, boxed board game, ca 1890, 7¼ x 7¼", 5 pieces [4 wooden counters and spinner], instructions on back of box cover, multicolored lithographed board, numbered, checkerboard type, track game **40.00**

Mother Goose Scroll Puzzle, puzzle, ©1882, 7½ x 9¾", several multicolored lithographed interlocking pieces, wooden box **100.00**

Naval Engagement, separate board and pieces box, 1870, 5½ x 9", opens to multicolored lithographed board as book, showing Civil War soldiers, cannon, water and ships **75.00**

New Game Familiar Quotations From Popular Authors, card game, ca 1895, 4½ x 6¼", 72 cards and instruction sheet, no illustrations **10.00**

New Game Of King's Quoits, boxed board game, ©1893, 16¾ x 18¾", 42 pieces [4 bone disks, 24 bone rings, 12 brass rings, 2 round felt mats], instructions on back of box cover, multicolored lithographed board has "court" pictures in each corner, attached red and blue pegs, 1½" w. partition on one side holds pieces, wooden box **275.00**

New Game Of Red Riding Hood, The, card game, ca 1888, 6¼ x 4 3/8", 42 multicolored lithographed cards and instruction booklet **30.00**

Old Fashioned Jack Straws, skill, ©1888, 6¼ x 4½", numerous wooden numbered pieces of different shapes and 2 hooks, instructions on back of box cover **20.00**

Old Fashioned Jack Straws, skill, ©1901, 5¼ x 7", several wooden numbered sticks of various shapes, 2 wooden handled hooks, direction sheet with date 1888 . . . . **20.00**

Old Maid, card game, ©1898, 3¼ x 4½", 42 pieces [40 cards, instruction sheet, advertising card] **20.00**

Picture Puzzle, "Early Rising", puzzle, ca 1885, 4¾ x 6¾", puzzle pieces are multicolored, lithographed, wooden and interlocking **50.00**

Quizzical Questions and Quaint Replies, card game, 1869, 2 5/8 x 2 1/8", 36 question and answer cards illustrated in black and white **55.00**

Tiddledy Winks, skill, ca 1890, 8¼ x 5", glass cup and 20 winks, instructions on back of box cover **20.00**

Where's Johnny, card game, ca 1899, 6¼ x 4½", 41 cards and instruction booklet, 22 are multicolored lithographed picture cards, 19 have lithographed borders and printed matter **35.00**

Yankee Pedlar, card game, ca 1865-70, 4 1/8 x 5 5/8", 12 lithographed hand-painted "merchant" cards, numerous small cards with printing, instruction booklet (which says "Yankee Pedler"), cover signed by lithographer Cogger S. C., game played like *Peter Coddles* **85.00**

Young Folks' Geographical Game, card game, ca 1895, 6¼ x 4½", 36 printed cards and instruction sheet, not illustrated **15.00**

METRO

Pimlico, separate board and pieces box, ca 1940, 4½ x 5½", 10 pieces [6 plastic horses' heads, 3 dice, instruction sheet], cardboard racetrack, green and tan, set in bottom of wood box, folding box top is leather with "Pimlico" written in script **20.00**

M. H. MILLER CO.

Jeannette, PA   ca 1910's

"Brownie" Kick-In Top, skill, ca 1910's 8½ x 8¾ x 1³/₈", metal bowl, (circular playing field), 2 piece spinning top, 5 wooden balls (1 colored, 4 white), instructions on box bottom **50.00**

CHAS. B. MUIR
(Polaris Company)

Washington, D.C.

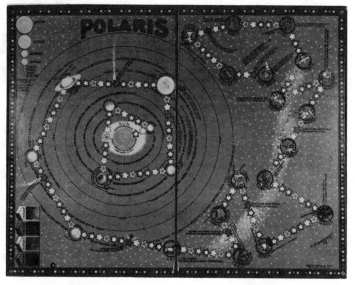

Polaris **65.00**

NATIONAL GAMES INC.

West Springfield, MA   ca 1930's

Triple Play, ca 1930's 9 x 11¼ x 1⅛" No.
D 3902 . . . .**10.00**

NATIONAL GOLF
SERVICE CO., INC.

New York, NY   ca 1920's

"Par' Golf Card Game, card game,
1926, 2¾ x 3⅝", 96 pieces [90 cards,
4 score cards, advertising card and instruction booklet], game invented by
Bert (Wheeler) Moorman, famous
comedian of "Wheeler and Woolsey"
team **125.00**

NATIONAL INDOOR GAME & NOVELTY CO.

Los Angeles, CA

World's Championship Baseball Game,
13 x 19" **125.00**

NATURE STUDY PUBLISHING CO.

ca 1890's

Birds, educational card game, ©1897,
2½ x 3½", 52 cards and instruction sheet, backs are brown and
white showing 2 birds in leaves,
faces are multicolored depicting different birds **30.00**

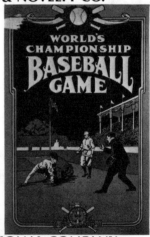

THE NEW CENTURY EDUCATIONAL COMPANY

New York, NY; Boston, MA   ca 1900

**New Century Busy Work-Wild Ani-
mals,** card game, ca 1900, 5½ x
4½", 25 pieces [16 card board photographs and paintings of animals, 8
small card board labels, instruction
sheet] **15.00**

NOBLE AND NOBLE PUBLISHERS, INC.

New York, NY

ca 1920's

Defenders Of The Flag,
ca 1922, 8¼ x 6⅛ x ¾", ... **35.00**

Three Bears, The,
1922, 8¼ x 6⅛ x ¾", ... **45.00**

HENRY D. NOYES & CO.

Boston, MA   ca 1870's

Old Hunter And His Game, The, card
game, ca 1870, 4¾ x 6½", 52 cards,
black and white, tan and white showing game, hunter and dogs, instruction
sheet **45.00**

NOYES & SNOW

Worcester, MA   ca 1870's

Successors to West & Lee Game Company.

"Game Of 76" Or The Lion & Eagle,
card game, 1876, 5⅞ x4¼", 50 cards
and instruction booklet, centennial
game **85.00**

Portrait Authors, card game, 1873, 4¼
x 6", 63 pieces [62 cards and instruction sheet] **15.00**

NOYES, SNOW & CO.

Boston, MA; Worcester, MA   ca 1870's

Successors to West & Lee Game Company.

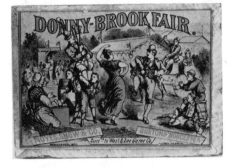 

Donny-Brook Fair, card game, 1877, 6¼ x 5¼", 104 pieces [65 small yellow squares, 7 animal cards, 31 people cards, instruction booklet] . . . **35.00**

Spella, educational, 1874, 5⅜ x 3⅜", 79 pieces [6 erasable tablets, 72 multicolored index word cards, instruction sheet] **30.00**

NUCRAFT TOYS

Wakefield, MA   ca 1920's

New Lindy Flying Game, The, card game, ©1927, 2¾ x 4", 79 cards and instruction sheet, card backs are green picturing 12 monoplanes, faces illustrated in black and white and red and white lithography, inventor is Paul K. Guillow **35.00**

THE NUMERICA CO.

ca 1890's

Game Of Numerica, card game, ©1894, 3¼ x 3¼", 210 pieces [208 numbered counters in 4 colors, picture

of family playing Numerica, instruction sheet] **15.00**

OFFSET-GRAVURE CORP.

New York, NY

ca 1930's

Trailer Trails With "Terry The Terrible Speed Cop", boxed board game, skill and chance, 1937, 9¼ x 14½", (incomplete—2 identical boards), blue, red, yellow and white **20.00**

OPTIMUS PRINTING COMPANY

New York, NY

ca 1900

Trusts and Busts, card game, ©1904, 2¾ x 3¾", 81 pieces [60 cards, 10 trust cards, 10 call cards, instruction sheet], backs rose and white depicting stock market scenes and say "Trusts and Busts of Frenzied Finance" **25.00**

J. OTTMANN LITH. CO.

New York, NY

ca 1890's-1910's

Commerce, ca 1900, 4⅝ x 6¼ x 1" **30.00**

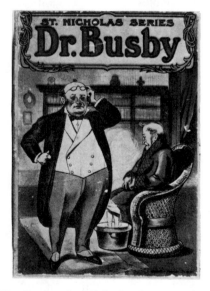

Dr. Busby, St. Nicholas Series, 6³/₈ x 8⅝" **25.00**

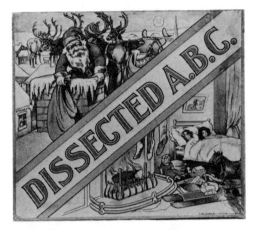

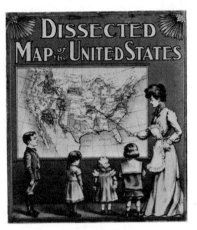

Dissected A.B.C., puzzle, ca 1910, 11½ x 10", 24 red, yellow and white puzzle pieces of alphabet **60.00**

Dissected Map Of The United States, puzzle, ca 1910, 10 x 11½", 20 lithographed multicolored puzzle pieces cut on straight lines . . **50.00**

Game Of Authors, card game, ca 1900, 5¼ x 7¼", 41 pieces [40 cards, instruction sheet], multicolored lithographed cards, letter series **20.00**

Peter Coddles, St. Nicholas Series, card game, ca 1890, 6¼ x 8¾", numerus printed cards and reading booklet **15.00**

GEORGE S. PARKER & CO.

Salem, MA ca 1880's

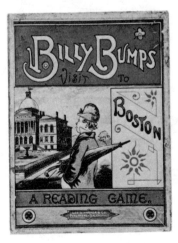

Billy Bumps Visit To Boston, card game, ca 1887, 4⅝ x 6¼", numerous printed cards and reading booklet, *Peter Coddles*-type game **25.00**

Johnny's Historical Game,
©1890 by Harry J. Phillips, 5¹/₁₆ x 6⁹/₁₆
x 1" **20.00**

**Chivalry, The Greatest Modern Board
Game Of Skill** **45.00**

Game Of Famous Men, The, card game,
ca 1887, 5⅝ x 4", 32 printed cards and
instruction sheet, played like Authors,
Game of Innocence Abroad advertised on box bottom **20.00**

When My Ship Comes In, card game,
©1888, 5½ x 4", 84 cards and instruction sheet, not illustrated **25.00**

**Ye Peculiar Game Of Ye Yankee Ped-
dler,** card game, ©1888, 6³/₈ × 4³/₄",
numerous printed cards and instruc-
tion sheet **30.00**

Ivanhoe, 1890, 6½ x 4½ x 1" . **20.00**

PARKER BROTHERS, INC.

Salem, MA; New York, NY; London, England   ca 1883-present

George S. Parker began the business in 1883, with his first game, *Banking*. Elder brother Charles joined him in 1888, and the firm became known as Parker Brothers. The eldest Parker brother, Edward H., joined the company in 1898. The three brothers incorporated in 1901. In 1968, Parker Brothers became a wholly owned subsidiary of General Mills. While the company's main plant remains in Salem, the executive offices have been located in Beverly, Massachusetts, since 1981. Parkers Brothers, Inc., has announced that the executive offices will return to Salem by January 1986.

Admiral Byrd's South Pole Game: "Little America", boxed board game, ca 1934, 17 x 13", 10 pieces [inserted board, 4 counters with attached microphones, 4 playing pieces, instruction sheet], board is multicolored map of South Pole, showing plane, penguins, icebergs, etc., track game . . . **300.00**

Amateur Golf, boxed board game, ©1928, 16 x 10", 58 pieces [52 cards, 4 pins, advertising sheet, instruction sheet], card backs are blue and white with scene of golfer hitting on course, board is multicolored, lithographed diagram of golf course **220.00**

Amusing Game Of Innocence Abroad, The, boxed board game, 1888, 19¼ x 10¼", 11 pieces [lift out folded board, block spinner, 8 colored wooden counters, instruction sheet], multicolored lithographed board opens to 18¾" square, depicts countryside, water, city, etc., with track running through all, game invented by Geo. S. Parker, before his brother joined him **345.00**

Baron Munchausen Game, The, pool, ©1933, 5 x 3½" 7+ pieces [dice cup, 5 wooden lettered dice, instruction sheet and a number of round green cardboard counters], based on comedy radio program **25.00**

138

Black Cat, The, card game, ©1897, 6½ x 5", 24 cards and instruction sheet, multicolored lithographed cards show cats in varied situations **50.00**

Boake Carter's Star Reporter Game, ca 1930's, 20 x 10³/₈ x 1⅝" **150.00**

Bowling: A Board Game, boxed board game, 1896, 15½ x 11½", spinner and 4 counters, instructions on back of box cover, board multicolored and lithographed, is pasted on inside box bottom, shows balls and ten pins, track game **140.00**

Boy Hunter, The, skill, ca 1925, 15¾ x 7", 13 pieces [4 cardboard targets on wooden supports, metal and wood rifle,

8 wooden pellets], instructions on back of box cover, targets are multicolored lithographed wild animals . . . **75.00**

Boy Scouts' Progress Game, The, boxed board game, 19 x 10"©1924-26, 88 pieces [80 counters or honors, 4 different colored wooden playing pieces, dice cup, 2 dice, instruction booklet and board], multicolored lithographed board folds in half, pictures scouts in each corner, track is comprised of the different scout badges; game is authorized by Boy Scouts of America **350.00**

Buffalo Hunt, ca 1890's 5¼ x 5¼ x6¾", board on bottom of box **30.00**

Bulls and Bears, separate board and pieces box, ©1936, 19″ square board, matching box (13½ × 6¾″) of 2 dice, instruction sheet, 6 wooden counters, 6 metal chairs, 9 certificates, stock pool cards and paper money, board folds in half and has multicolored tracks **85.00**

Buzzing Around, skill game, ca 1924, 10³/₈″ square, 6 pieces [lift out board, spring top, 4 colored wooden counters], instructions on back of box cover, fenced-in board, divided into 4 colored squares, each with standing pin **40.00**

Calling All Cars, boxed board game, ca 1938, 16 x 8″, 7 pieces [green double spinner, 4 colored metal cars, board which folds in half, instruction sheet], box bottom partitioned to hold cars **55.00**

Captain Kidd, boxed board game, ©1896, 16½ x 14½″, 5 pieces [4 cardboard sailing ships in colored, wooden supports, and spinner], instructions on back of box cover, multicolored lithographed board shows water, fort, pirates and beach and wharf, wooden box, track game **475.00**

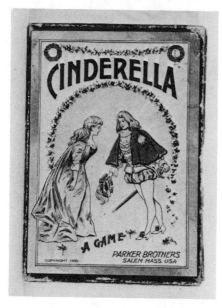

Captain Kidd Junior, boxed board game, 1926, 10¾ x 12", 27 pieces [dice cup, 2 dice, 24 colored wooden counters], instructions on back of box cover, board insert, multicolored lithographed scene of pirates, ship, etc., track game . . . . ©**85.00**

Cinderella, card game, ©1895, 4 x 5½", 25 multicolored lithographed cards and instruction sheet **20.00**

Comical Game Of "Who", The, card game, ca 1910, 6½ x 5", 60 printed cards and instruction sheet, not illustrated **20.00**

Comical Game: Sir Hinkle Funny-Duster, The, card game ©1903, 5¼ x 6¾", 20 multicolored lithographed cards and instruction sheet, game played like *Happy Families* . . **25.00**

Comical History Of America, card game, ca 1920's, 7³/₈ x 4¾ x 1" **25.00**

Cones and Corns, skill, ©1924, 8⅝ x 3⅞", 30 pieces [8 colored wooden sticks, 4 colored wooden cone receptacles, 18 colored wooden "acorn" pieces], instructions on back of box cover **25.00**

Contack, domino type game, ©1939, 6½ x 3⅞ x 1¼", 36 triangular pieces, score cards, red, white, and blue chips, 12 pages, 3⁵⁄₁₆ x 3⅞", instruction booklet **10.00**

County Fair, The, card game, ©1891, 6⅜ x 4⅝", 24 character cards, numerous numbered price cards, and instruction sheet **25.00**

Crossing The Ocean, boxed board game, ©1893, 14¾ x 8⅞", 4 colored wooden counters, instructions on back of box cover, multicolored lithographed board depicts water surrounded by famous world ports, and has spinner affixed in lower right corner . . . **140.00**

142

Crows in The Corn, skill, ©1930, 13¾ x 12⅛″, instructions on back of box cover, multicolored lithographed wooden and cardboard target of crows on fence, gun with pellets . . . **110.00**

"Derby Day" card game, ca 1900, 2½ x 3¾″, 48 multicolored lithographed cards, instruction booklet, many red and black numbered cardboard chips **35.00**

Dewey's Victory, boxed board game, ©1900, 16½ x 14½″, 14 pieces [7 yellow and 6 blue, round cardboard disks, spinner], instructions on back of box cover, multicolored lithographed board depicts water mass, which is checkered, and surrounding towns and landscape, wooden box, strategy game **475.00**

Dig, ©1940, 10⅞ x 7⅜ x 1⅜″, pile of letters, 4 picks, calling cards, shares, gold bars, instruction sheet, 2 sides, 3⅞ x 6⅞″, additional instructions on inside of lid **35.00**

Doctors and The Quack, card game, ca 1887, 6½ x 4⅞", numerous printed cards, not illustrated, on back of box bottom is advertisement for *Chivalry* **35.00**

Eddie Cantor's New Game, "Tell It to the Judge", separate board and pieces, box 19¾" square, ©1936 5⅞ x 10¾" matching box of 106+ [15 wooden counters, "Judge" label, 2 dice, 88 cards, paper "fine" money and instruction sheet], board multicolored lithographed track **25.00**

Dodging Donkey, The, skill, ca 1924, 7⅛ x 13¾", instructions on back of box cover, multicolored lithographed hanging donkey in barn target with 4 colored balls **75.00**

Fairies' Cauldron Tiddledy Winks Game, The, skill, ca 1925, 7¼ x 4¼", 16 pieces [2 felts, 3 sticks, base and black wooden bucket to make cauldron, 10 colored bone winks, and instruction sheet] **30.00**

Five Wise Birds, The, skill, ca 1920's, 17½ x 8¼ x 1¼" **45.00**

Flying The United States Air Mail, boxed board game, ©1929, 18 x 14½", 9+ pieces [lift out board, 4 colored metal airplanes, dice cup, 2 dice, numerous white printed cards, representing mail, and instruction sheet], folding board, multicolored, lithographed, opens to 28 x 17¼", is map of U.S., track game **200.00**

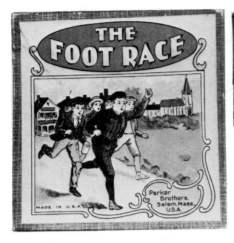

Fun At The Zoo: A Game, boxed board game, ©1902, 21 x 11", 7 pieces [6 colored wooden markers and spinner], instructions on back of box cover, multicolored lithographed board pictures many animals of zoo with track running through, wooden box . **240.00**

Foot Race, The, boxed board game, ca 1900, 5³/₈" square, 7 pieces [4 round colored wooden counters, spinner, 2 advertising cards], instructions on back of box cover, multicolored lithographed board represents simple track **15.00**

Game Of American History, The, card game, ca 1890, 8¼ x 5½", 60 cards and instruction sheet, not illustrated **35.00**

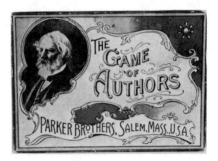

Fortune Telling Game, The, card game, ca 1890, 4¾ x 6¼", 30 cards and instruction sheet, 20 cards are printed, 10 are black and white lithographed illustrations **25.00**

Game Of Authors, The, card game ca 1890, 5½ x 3⁷/₈", 28 cards and instruction sheet, black and white lithographed portraits of famous authors **15.00**

Game of Boy Scouts, The, card game, ©1912, 5½ x 4", 50 cards and instruction sheet, card backs show scouts holding flags, faces are in different colors and 10 of one color design form a patrol, additional 2 advertising cards **75.00**

Game Of Buffalo Bill, The, boxed board game, ©1898, 15 x 9", 5 pieces [4 colored wooden counters and spinner], instructions on back of box cover, multicolored lithographed board depicts Indians, buffalo and Buffalo Bill, track game **185.00**

Game Of Bunny Rabbit, The, boxed board game, ca 1928-29, 9 x 17", 9 pieces [dice cup, 2 dice, 4 metal playing pieces (2 rabbits and 2 foxes), instruction sheet, board], board multicolored lithographed, has foxes chasing rabbits in center, track game .. **110.00**

Game Of Camouflage, The, card game, ca 1915-18, $6\frac{5}{8}$ x $3\frac{7}{8}$", 58 pieces [56 cards, spinner and instruction sheet], backs are blue and white and picture cannon and World War I soldiers **25.00**

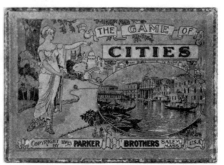

Game Of Cities, The, card game
©1893, 5⅝ × 4 × ¾″ **25.00**

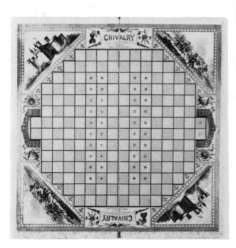

Game Of Fame, The, card game, ca
1901, 6½ × 5″, 40 printed cards and
instruction sheet, not illustrated **20.00**

Game Of Chivalry, The, boxed board
game, ©1888, 15¾″ square, 40
wooden pieces in red and yellow and
instruction booklet, multicolored lithographed board depicts castles and
knights in each corner, is checkered
and 2 drawers holding game pieces are
built in at each side, game invented by
George S. Parker and was his favorite,
although it was never a success,
strategy game **550.00**

Game Of Jack-Straws, The, skill, ca
1888, 5½ × 4″, numerous wooden
colored sticks of different shapes, and
wooden and metal hook **20.00**

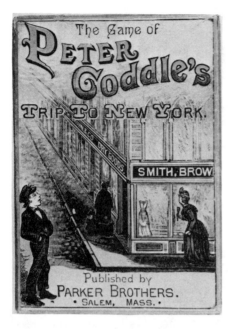

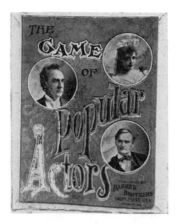

Game Of Popular Actors, The, card game, ©1893, 5³⁄₈ x 6⁵⁄₈″, 36 cards, instruction sheet and advertising sheet, cards are photographs of many old-time theater and Vaudeville actors and actresses, including Julia Marlowe, Lily Langtry, Joseph Jefferson, Edwin Booth, etc. **75.00**

Game Of Peter Coddles, The, card game, ca 1888, 4 x 5½″, numerous printed cards and reading booklet titled "Peter Codles" **20.00**

Game Of Ports and Commerce, The, ©1899, 5½ x 4″, 52 cards with instruction sheet and 1 advertising card, cards have black and white photos on faces, and red and white backs **25.00**

Game Of Red Riding-Hood, Adventure Series, boxed board game, ca 1895, 20¼ x 10³⁄₈″, spinner and 2 colored wooden counters, instructions on back of box cover, multicolored lithographed board shows Red Riding Hood, Wolf and lumbermen along track winding through forest **425.00**

Game Of Politics **30.00**

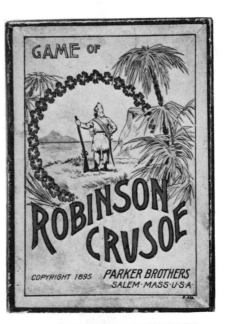

Game Of Red Riding Hood, boxed board game, ©1895, 9½ x 6½", 4 pieces [2 colored wooden counters, spinner and lift out board], instructions on back of box cover, multicolored lithographed board shows Red Riding Hood's path through the forest, grandmother, wolf, etc. **120.00**

Game Of Rich Uncle **40.00**

Game Of Robinson Crusoe, card game, ©1895, 3⅞ x 5½", 33 multicolored lithographed cards and instruction sheet, played like *Old Maid* . **25.00**

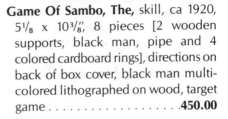

Game Of Sambo, The, skill, ca 1920, 5⅛ x 10⅜", 8 pieces [2 wooden supports, black man, pipe and 4 colored cardboard rings], directions on back of box cover, black man multi-colored lithographed on wood, target game **450.00**

Game Of Shopping, The, card game, ca 1888, 3¾ x 5½", numerous "merchandise" cards, 36 small price cards, and instruction sheet **35.00**

Game Of Snap, The, card game, ca 1885, 20 multicolored lithographed cards and instruction sheet; played like *Happy Families* **45.00**

Game Of Steeple Chase, "Tom Thumb" Edition, boxed board game, ca 1895, 9½ x 6½", 4 colored wooden counters, multicolored lithographed lift out board depicts race track, has spinner affixed in center, and instructions printed around sides **65.00**

Game Of Steeple Chase, The, Popular Edition, boxed board game, ca 1895, 14⅞ x 8⅞", 5 pieces [4 round colored wooden markers and spinner], instructions on back of box cover, multicolored lithographed board shows race track with horses leaping over obstacle in center, and horses in each corner **125.00**

Game Of Ten Little Niggers, The, card game, ca 1895, 5¾ x 4¼", 21 multicolored lithographed cards, all dealing with blacks, and instruction sheet, played like *Old Maid* . **400.00**

Game Of Travel, boxed board game, ©1894, 20½ x 13½", board is boxed in wood and has pull out drawer containing 29 pieces [25 cards, spinner, 2 metal ships, instruction sheet], pasted ad on inside drawer states "The Parker Game Board. Patented Oct. 2, 1894. Took Highest Awards, World's Columbian Exposition, Chicago, 1893." **450.00**

Game Of "Uncle Sam's Farm", card game, ©1895, 6½ x 5", 35 multicolored lithographed cards and instruction sheet, cards depict well known scenic locations in the U.S. **35.00**

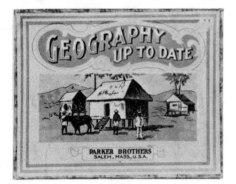

Geography Up To Date, educational card game, ca 1890, 6¾ x 5¼", 48 cards, advertising card, and instruction sheet, not illustrated **15.00**

George Washington's Dream, card game, ca 1899, 7½ x 4⅝", numerous colored printed cards, advertising card, and instruction and reading booklet, played like *Peter Coddles* **20.00**

Gold Hunters, The, boxed board game, ca 1902, 13¾" square, 5 pieces [4 colored wooden counters and spinner], instructions on back of box cover, multicolored lithographed board depicts trails in Alaska, over Yukon and Klondike Rivers, and mountains, track game **195.00**

Hand Of Fate, The, fortune telling game, ca 1910, 13¼ x 11½ x 1¼", . . . **55.00**

Hen That Laid The Golden Egg, The, boxed board game, ©1900, 14½ x 16½", 29 pieces [spinner, 4 hens, 24 eggs], instructions on back of cover, game board on box bottom, multicolored, lithographed, 24 nests on gold circular ground, baskets of eggs in corners, wooden box **275.00**

Hickety Pickety, boxed board game, 1924, 10¾ x 12", 25 pieces [multicolored lithographed board with spinner in center, 6 wooden yellow eggs, 6 wooden red eggs, 6 blue eggs, 6 wooden green eggs], instructions on back of box cover **40.00**

Hidden Titles, card game, ca 1910's 6½ x 5⅛ x 1" **15.00**

History Up To Date, card game, ca 1904, 6¾ x 5¼", 48 cards, advertising card and instruction sheet, cards not illustrated, believe this to be earlier game that was updated **25.00**

Hokum, card game, ©1927, 8¼ x 6¼", 8 numbered cards, numerous numbered yellow disks, and many round red markers, game played like *Bingo*................ **15.00**

"Hold The Fort", boxed board game, ©1895, 15¼ x 13", 53 colored wooden counters, multicolored lithographed board 12½ x 13", 2" partition to hold pieces, instructions on back of box cover, board is lined and checkered with Civil War battlescenes in 2 corners, eagle in third, and flags in fourth, wooden box........ **275.00**

House That Jack Built, The, card game, ca 1890, 6 x 4¾", 16 color lithographed cards, instruction sheet, played like *Old Maid*........ **20.00**

How Silas Popped The Question, card game, ca 1915, 6½ x 5", 35 printed cards and reading booklet, *Peter Coddles*-type game; no logo on box cover but 2 *Parker Brothers, Inc.* ads in box **20.00**

Jack and Jill, boxed board game, ca 1892, 15 x 9", 2 wooden counters and spinner, instructions on back of box cover, multicolored lithographed board shows path winding from thatched cottage, up hill dotted with sheep, to well house, Jack and Jill pictured in lower right corner, but as much younger children than on cover **125.00**

Jack and The Beanstalk, boxed board game, ©1895, 9½ x 6½", 2 wooden counters and spinner, multicolored lithographed lift out board shows Giant, Jack, castle, Jack's home and hen with golden eggs, directions printed on all sides of board, track game . . . **40.00**

Jolly Old Maid, The, card game, ca 1910, 4¾ x 6", 23 multicolored lithographed cards, instruction card, and 2 advertisement sheets **20.00**

Knockout Andy, skill, 1926, 8³/₈ x 8³/₈", 10 pieces [red wooden board with 4 pegs, 8 green wooden bowling pins, multicolored metal and wood spring top], instructions on back of box cover **40.00**

Komical Konversation Kards, card game, ©1893, 5 x 6½", numerous question and answer cards and instruction sheet, not illustrated **20.00**

Letters Or Anagrams, classic, ca 1889, 5½ x 4", numerous round pink lettered disks and instruction sheet . . . **20.00**

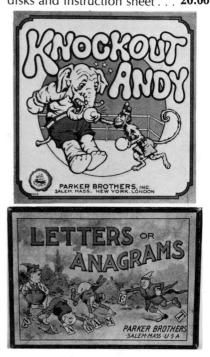

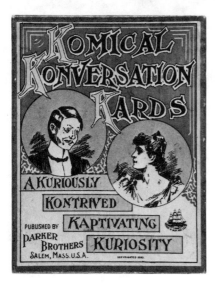

Lindy, card game, ©1927, 2¾ x 4⅛″, 99 cards and instruction sheet, cards have pink backs and are illustrated in black and white lithography on faces **25.00**

Lindy, Improved Edition, card game, ©1927, 5½ x 4″, 99 cards, advertising sheet and instruction sheet, card backs are blue and white, picturing 5 planes, faces illustrated in black and white lithography **25.00**

Literary Salad, card game, ©1890, 6½ x 5″, 48 cards and instruction sheet, not illustrated, played like *Authors,* older game in updated box **20.00**

Literary Salad, card game, ©1890, 5¼″ square, 36 cards and instruction sheet, not illustrated, played like *Authors* **20.00**

Little Bo-Peep, card game, ©1895, 5½ × 4″, 28 multicolored lithographed cards with instruction sheet . . . **20.00**

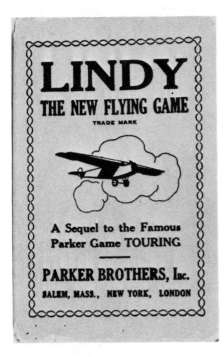

Little Cowboy Game, The, boxed board game, ca 1895, 20½ x 10½", 5 pieces [4 round colored wooden counters and spinner], instructions on back of box cover, multicolored lithographed board has checkered oval track with cowboy and steer pictured in center, cowboy motif not common in old games, wooden box **375.00**

Little Mother Goose, card game, ca 1890, 5¾ x 4¼", 33 cards and instruction card, card backs are pink, faces are multicolored lithographed illustrations **30.00**

Little People's Picture Puzzle, puzzle, ©1915, 12¾ x 9", 2 puzzles, multicolored and lithographed, signed by Alice Hirschberg **75.00**

Little Pigs, The, boxed board game, ca 1890, 10 x 7", 17 pieces [16 round colored wooden counters and spinner], instructions on back of box cover, multicolored lithographed board shows pig in each corner and circular track in center **150.00**

Little Red Bushy-Tail, separate board and pieces box, ©1921, 18½" square board, matching box of playing pieces [4 wooden counters, numerous numbered cards, and instruction booklet], multi-colored lithographed track board with animal figures, folds in half . . **50.00**

Lone Ranger Game, The, separate board and pieces box, ©1938, multicolored lithographed 18½" square board, 5 x 7½" matching box of 17 playing pieces [2 spinner cards, 4 colored metal rearing horse figures, 10 markers (2 red plastic and 8 metal), instruction sheet], board folds in half **60.00**

London Game, The, boxed board game, ©1898, 25 x 16½", 8+ pieces [2 dice cups, 4 dice, 4 colored wooden markers and package of toy letters], instructions on back of box cover, multicolored lithographed board represents detailed map of London, wooden box; had both British and American patents **825.00**

Man Hunt, board game, 1937, 17½ x 14 x 1½", cards with character descriptions of fictional criminals . . . **45.00**

Mansion Of Happiness, The, boxed board game, ©1894, 21 x 14", [spinner and 6 colored wooden counters], instructions on back of box cover, multicolored lithographed board is affixed to top of box bottom, with pull out drawer in side for gaming pieces, oval track with picture of mansion in center, wooden box; this is Parker Brothers reissue of the early (1843) game by W. & S. B. Ives **475.00**

Monopoly, board game, first edition, 1935 . . . . **35.00**

Monopoly, Popular Edition, board game, 1936 . . . . **25.00**

The National-American Baseball Game **75.00**

News Boy, The, boxed board game, ©1895, 7½" square, 6 pieces [lift out board, spinner, 4 colored wooden counters], multicolored lithographed board has instructions printed along all 4 sides, track game **40.00**

Office Boy, The, boxed board game, ©1889, 18 x 10", 6 pieces [lift out folded board, 4 lead office boys and block spinner], multicolored lithographed board opens to 19¼ x 17½", pictures of office in center and in 3 corners, instructions printed on board in lower left corner, track game **500.00**

Old Glory, card game, ©1899, 4 x 5½", 52 cards and 2 advertising cards, all with colored U.S. flag backs, cards picture U.S. military heroes, played like *Authors* **40.00**

Old Woman Who Lived In A Shoe, The, boxed board game, ca 1895, 8 x 13", 17 pieces [16 round colored wooden markers and spinner], instructions on back of box cover, multicolored lithographed checkered board shows Old Woman in Shoe in center . . . **110.00**

Parker Brothers Post Office Game,
educational, 9 x 11¾", ca 1910, box bottom outfitted for child to play post office with postman's mask, cancel stamp, several sheets of stationery and envelopes, sets of Santa Claus sets, and several post cards **325.00**

Peg Top, 12 x 10¾" **25.00**

Peggy, boxed board game, ©1923, 12 x 10¾", 21 pieces [20 colored wooden pegs and wooden spinning top], instructions on back of box cover, multicolored lithographed board looks exactly like cover **75.00**

Peg'ity, boxed board game, ca 1925, 10¼ x 13½", numerous pegs in colors in partitions above and under gray cardboard holed board, instructions on back of box cover, strategy game **35.00**

161

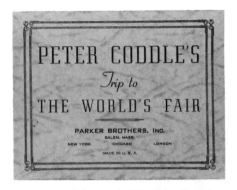

Peter Coddle and His Trip To New York, card game, ca 1901, 4 × 5½″, printed cards, reading booklet   **15.00**

Peter Coddle Tells Of His Trip To Chicago, card game, ca 1890, 5⅞ × 4⅜″, numerous printed cards and reading booklet **15.00**

Peter Coddle's Trip To New York, Nickel Edition, classic, ca 1920's, 3⅜ × 4⅝ × ¾″, 18 cards with 3 phrases per card, 4 page 3 × 4″ instruction book with story containing blanks **15.00**

Peter Coddle's Trip To The World's Fair, 1939, 6⅝ × 5⅛ × 1″ **10.00**

Philo Vance, board game, 1937, 19¼ × 9⅞ × 1⅞″, created by S. S. VanDine die cast metal pawns, dice, pictorial object cards **60.00**

"Pike's Peak or Bust", puzzle, ©1895, 7½" square, instructions written in red on top of board, which has lithographed blue mountain peaks studded with metal pegs, attached to base is string tied to metal "scaler"; patented by Judson M. Fuller **95.00**

Ping Pong, skill, ca 1904, 16⅞ x 7³/₈", 13 pieces [4 wooden sand paper-coated paddles, 6 celluloid balls, net, 2 metal net holders, instruction booklet]; Parker's first Ping Pong game after negotiating with rights from Britain, balls still marked "Match-England" **120.00**

Polly Pickles: The Great Movie Game: A Burlesque, board and pieces box, ©1921, board: 18⅞ x 19", pieces box: 5¹/₈ x 3³/₈ x 2", 12 pieces [game board, dice cup, 6 movie dice, 4 playing pieces], 4 page 3¾ x 4⁵/₈" instruction booklet, supplemental instruction sheet, round track gameboard with 105 stops, multicolored, humorous movie theme, dice each have 6 letters, turned wood playing pieces **75.00**

Popular Game Of Ludo, The, boxed board game, ca 1890, 13⁵/₈" square, 19 pieces [dice cup, 2 dice, 16 round colored wooden counters], multicolored lithographed board, with shields in each corner, track game played like *Parcheesi* **85.00**

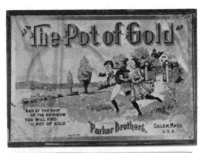

Popular Jack-Straw, skill, ca 1888, 4½ x 6¼", numerous wooden numbered sticks of different shapes, 2 hooks, and instruction sheet **20.00**

Postman Game, The, boxed board game, ca 1895, 5¼" square, 4 round wooden colored markers and die, multicolored lithographed board is simple track **15.00**

Pot Of Gold, The,©1897, 17 x 11½", 6 pieces [4 wooden counters, spinner, instruction sheet], board pasted on bottom of box, multicolored lithograph shows rainbow with pot of gold at end, track game **125.00**

Professional Game Of Base Ball, The, boxed board game, ca 1889, 8¼" square, 8 round colored wooden counters and 2 dice, instructions on back of box cover, multicolored lithographed board represents baseball diamond, ... **75.00**

Quick Wit, card game, ©1938, 5¼ x 3⅞ x 1⅝", cartoon cover by Gluyas Williams, [editions without Williams cover, **10.00**] **15.00**

Quien Sabe, card game, ©1906, 5¼ x 3½", 120 cards, advertising sheet and instruction sheet, lettered red and white backs show Spanish cowboy on

164

bucking horse, faces are green and white, numbered, showing cowboy roping **20.00**

Quiz Kids Own Game Box, ©1940, 17⅛ x 9 x 1½″ **20.00**

Ring The Pin, skill, ca 1910, 9½ x 6½″, 22 pieces [target on wooden supports, piece of felt, 4 colored bone squares, and 16 colored bone rings], instructions on back of box cover, target is multicolored and lithographed with metal hooks **35.00**

Rip-Van Win-kle, boxed board game, ca 1890, 15 x 9″, 5 pieces [4 colored wooden counters and spinner], instructions on back of box cover, multicolored lithographed board shows track winding through scenes of Van Winkle waking up under tree, mountain folk bowling, his wife scolding, etc. . . **125.00**

Siege Of Havana, The, boxed board game, ©1898, 22½ x 16¼″, 9+ pieces [4 colored metal battleships, dice cup, 3 dice, spinner, and numerous colored wooden "shot" and shells], instructions on back of box cover, board is affixed to top of box bottom with pull out drawer for playing pieces, multicolored lithographed board depicts water Havana, Morro Castle, batteries, cannon and ships, wooden box, track game **550.00**

Street Car Game, The, boxed board game, ca 1892, 15 x 9″, 9 pieces [8 round colored wooden markers and spinner], instructions on back of box cover, multicolored lithographed board simulates city street map on which trolley tracks run **425.00**

That's Me!, ca 1937, 18¼ x 9½ x 2⅛" **15.00**

Toot, card game ©1905, 5½ x 4", 76 cards and instruction sheet, card backs are red and white, faces picture old time auto in red, blue, orange, and green **25.00**

Touring, card game, ©1926, 5¼ x 4", 99 cards and instruction sheet, cards have red and white backs with touring car pictured in center, faces are illustrated in black and white lithography . . **25.00**

Tox, boxed board game, 1894, 8½" square, instructions on back of box cover, multicolored lithographed numbered board pasted on inside of box bottom, 25 round wooden numbered counters, board has "Brownie"-like figures around border **35.00**

Toy-Town Telegraph Office, educational, ca 1910, 9⅜ x 13⅞", 16+ pieces [2 Western Union boy masks, 2 office windows, 4 wooden supports for windows, 2 wooden telegraph keys, ink pad, packet of toy money, pad of cablegrams, pad of telegrams, pad of night letters, and several Western Union envelopes], instructions on back of cover, including Morse Code **325.00**

Train for Boston, boxed board game, ©1900, 16½ x 14½", 5 pieces [4 colored wooden counters and spinner], instructions on back of box cover, multicolored lithographed board shows stations of Washington, St. Louis, Chicago and New York in each corner and Boston right of center, wooden box, track game **1250.00**

Trip Around The World, A, ca 1920, 16¾ x 11½ x 1½" **55.00**

Twentieth Century Limited, ca 1910, 21½ x 14½ x 1", wooden box **425.00**

Walt Disney's Uncle Remus Game, ca 1930's, 17½ x 10 x 1¾" **125.00**

Watermelon Puzzle, puzzle, ©1896, 7½" square, instructions on back of box cover, 55 wooden markers, multicolored lithographed checkered board with picture of black man in center **125.00**

What Color Is Your Car?, quiz, ©1923, 7½ x 4¾", several score cards, story book, and instruction booklet . **25.00**

Wings, card game, ©1928, 5½ x 4", No. 789, 99 cards and instruction booklet, card backs are pink and white, picturing air mail plane, faces illustrated in black and white lithography . **20.00**

Winnie-The-Pooh Game, ©1933, by Stephen Slesinger, Inc., 17⅛ x 8⅞ x 7¹/₁₆" **65.00**

Winnie-The-Pooh, boxed board game, ©1933, 17 x 9", 9 pieces [4 cardboard counters in wooden supports, multicolored lithographed board which folds in half, cloth bag containing numerous colored markers, instruction sheet], multicolored advertising circular] **75.00**

Wogglebug Game of Conundrums, The, card game, ©1905, 6½ x 5", numerous question and answer cards of gray and buff, advertising sheet and instruction sheet, cards not illustrated; because Wogglebug was character in Oz books, this game is sought after by Wizard of Oz buffs **95.00**

Wonderful Game of Oz, The boxed
board game, ©1921, 10 x 19", 11 pieces
[dice cup, 6 wooden 'Wizard' cubes,
4 pewter figures of Dorothy and friends,
instruction booklet, and board], board
is multicolored, lithographed map,
track game; the earlier game had
the pewter figures, later, Parker used
plain wood disks, so the first is more
valuable **950.00**

Yankee Doodle, boxed board game,
©1895, 21¼ x 14⅛", 5+ pieces [spin-
ner, 4 colored wooden counters, many
red and yellow cardboard disks], directions on back of box cover, multicolored lithographed board shows
pictures of historic naval engagements and battles of U.S. history,
wooden box **625.00**

Across The Continent, boxed board game, ca 1935, 18 x 11¼", 36 pieces [board, 4 dice cups, 8 dice, 4 colored metal trains (made by Tootsie Toy) 18 tickets, and instruction sheet], multicolored lithographed board folded in three sections, opens to 32½ x 17¼" and is map of U. S. **125.00**

Airship Game, The, card game, 1916, 7½ x 5½", 56 cards and instruction sheet, cards have blue and white backs depicting early aircraft, faces show monoplanes, biplanes, zeppelins, and balloons in red and white . . . **40.00**

Apple Pie, card game, ©1895, 5½ x 4", 25 pieces [5 cardboard wedges of pie, 20 black and white cards illustrated with knife or fork, and instruction sheet] **15.00**

Bargain Day, 9½ x 9½" **30.00**

Baseball Game, card game, ©1913, $5^3/_8$ x $3^7/_8$", 52 pieces [50 cards, folding baseball diamond playing board, instruction sheet], card backs are red and white with picture of Cleveland player (Tris Speaker?) **55.00**

Barber Pole, skill, ca 1900, $6^1/_8$ x $6^1/_8$ x $2^3/_8$", wooden barber pole $5^5/_8$" high with 8 hooks on it, 4 felt pads, 4 square bone pieces (tiddley winks), 8 bone kings, instructions inside box lid **25.00**

Barn Yard Tiddledy Winks, skill, ca 1910, $11^5/_8$ x $7^5/_8$", 14+ pieces [1 multicolored lithographed barnyard fenced in by wooden fence, 12 multicolored lithographed farm animal figures with wooden supports, round felt, and several colored bone "winks", instructions on back of box cover . . **40.00**

Block, Parker Brothers, card game, ©1905, $5^3/_8$ x $3^7/_8$", 56 cards and instruction sheet, game invented by George S. Parker, and won Grand Prize at St. Louis World's Fair, 1904 . . . . . **15.00**

Broadway, separate board and pieces box, 1917, 17¾" square board, matching box of 23 pieces [2 dice, 2 dice cups, 16 colored brass-bound disks, instruction sheet], board folds in half and is multicolored track similar to that of *Pollyanna,* shows New York City in each corner **35.00**

Camelot, separate board and pieces box, ©1930, 19 x 16¾" board, $4^5/_8$ x $6^1/_8$" matching box of 30 pieces [28 wooden counters, advertising sheet, instruction booklet], board folds in half, modern version of *Chivalry,* George S. Parker's favorite game **30.00**

Captain Jinks, card game, ca 1899, $3^3/_8$ x $4^5/_8$", 19 multicolored lithographed cards, instructions on back of box cover, played like *Old Maid* . . **15.00**

Coon Hunt Game, The, boxed board game, 1903, $14^7/_8$ x 9½", 2 colored wooden counters and spinner, instructions on back of box cover, multicolored lithographed board shows picture of black "Uncle Rastus" in top center, with three other pictures of coon dogs, track game **250.00**

Crazy Traveller, skill ca 1920, 12¼" square, 8 pieces [12" square, wooden and sided board with 8 pegs affixed, 6 wooden ten pins and spring top], instructions on back of box cover **30.00**

Cube Anagrams, educational, 1899, 7½ x 4", 11 pieces [2 dice cups, 6 wooden lettered dice, instruction sheet], like today's *Boggle* **15.00**

Excuse Me!, card game, ©1923, 7½ x 4¾", 124 printed pink and white cards and instruction sheet, not illustrated **15.00**

Game of Anagrams, The, educational ca 1910, 6¾ x 9¾", numerous wooden lettered blocks, and instruction sheet **10.00**

Game of Authors, The, card game, ca 1890, 4¼ x 5¾", No. 372, 30 cards and instruction sheet **10.00**

Game Of Authors, The, card game, ©1893, 6¼ x 4¾", 52 cards, 2 advertising cards, instruction sheet, cards have red and white backs and lithographed, black and white portraits of famous authors **10.00**

Game Of Favorite Art, ©1897, 9½ x 6½", 64 cards and instruction sheet, cards are photographed works of great artists, wooden box **40.00**

Game of Flags, educational card game, 1915, 8 x 4", 52 multicolored lithographed flag cards, numerous yellow card board counters and instruction booklet **20.00**

Game of International Authors, The, card game, ©1893, 30 cards and instruction sheet **10.00**

Game of Jack Straws, The, skill, ca 1895, 7½ x 5½", 2 hooks and numerous numbered natural wood pieces of different shapes **15.00**

Game Of Snap, The, card game, ca 1889, 4 x 5½", 18 multicolored lithographed cards and instruction card . . . **15.00**

Good Old Game of Innocence Abroad, The, boxed board game, ©1888, 18 x 20", 8 pieces [6 colored wooden counters, spinner, instruction sheet], multicolored lithographed board is set in and attached to box bottom, 1³/₈" w. partition on one side holds

playing pieces, wooden box, track game; believe this to be later edition of original game (1888) because of Incorporation **250.00**

Good Old Game Of Dr. Busby, card game, ca 1903-05, 7½ x 5½", 20 multicolored lithographed cards and instruction sheet **25.00**

Hidden Titles, card game, ca 1910, 6³/₈ x 5", 30 cards and instruction sheet, cards are lithographed illustrations in black and white and are actually rebuses **20.00**

Hop Scotch Tiddledy Winks, skill, 1891, 10¼ x 6¾", 25 pieces [1 cup, 20 winks, 2 felt pads, advertising sheet, instruction sheet], 1 felt, red and yellow, with bullseye, other felt is hopscotch court **20.00**

I Doubt It, card game, ca 1910, 6½ x 5", 48 cards, advertising sheet, and instruction sheet, cards are numbered with blue and white backs **15.00**

Japanola, skill, 1928, 11½ x 13¾", 7 pieces [wooden board with 6 depressions that lifts out, 6 colored wooden balls, 1¾" in diameter], instructions on back of box cover **25.00**

Kindergarten Drawing Teacher, art, ca 1900, 7 x 9½", 25 pieces [24 stencils and instruction sheet] **25.00**

Lame Duck, The, boxed board game, ©1928, 17 x 9", No. 508, 6 pieces [4 colored celluloid ducks, duck spinner and folding lift out board], instructions on back of box cover, multicolored lithographed board opens to 16½" square, pictures duck pond with ducks in each corner, track game **50.00**

Lindy Hop-Off, boxed board game, ©1920, 14½ x 13½", 25 pieces [2 dice cups, 2 dice, 16 cards, 4 metal colored planes, instruction sheet], lift out, folding, multicolored lithographed board opens to 25¾ x 12¾", pictures same plane on cover flying ocean between maps of North America and Europe, this 1920 game obviously had the word "Lindy" added to its title after Lindbergh's flight in 1927. . . .**350.00**

Mrs. Casey Wants To Know, card game, ca 1910, 6½ x 5", numerous question and answer cards and instruction sheet, not illustrated **15.00**

Multicolor Ten Pins, skill, ca 1922, 14¾ x 4¼", 13 pieces [10 colored wooden pins, 3¾" tall, 3 colored wooden balls, 1½" in diameter] **35.00**

My Mother Sent Me To The Grocery Store, card game, ca 1902, 6½ x 5", 20 illustrated black and white cards, numerous blue "product" slips, and instruction sheet **20.00**

New Testament, The, Game Of Quotations, card game, ca 1920's, 5¹/₁₆ x 6⁷/₁₆ x 1¹/₁₆" **10.00**

Old Maid Game, card game, ca 1910, 7½ x 5½", 37 multicolored lithographed cards with pink backs, and instruction sheet **20.00**

Parker Brothers Game Of Birds, card game, ca 1904, 8 x 4", 52 multicolored lithographed cards of different birds, instruction sheet, 2 advertising cards **25.00**

Parker Brothers Game Of Flowers, card game, ca 1915, 8 x 3⁷/₈", 52 cards, 2 advertising cards, and instruction sheet, cards are multicolored lithographed pictures of different flowers **25.00**

Parker Brothers' United States Puzzle Map, puzzle, ©1915, 12¾ x 7¾", model map in black and white on back of box cover, multicolored lithographed puzzle pieces of U.S. map **30.00**

Peg Base Ball, boxed board game, ca 1924, 12 x 10¾", No. 587, 15 pieces [12 colored wooden pegs, dice cup, 2 dice], instructions on back of box cover **30.00**

Pepper, ca1900, 6⁵/₈ x 5¹/₈ x 1" . **15.00**

Pick-A-Peg, skill, ©1928, 13¼ x 11½" No. 782; 8 pieces [4 colored wooden pegs, 4 colored wooden poles with metal disks attached by string], instructions on back of box cover, multicolored lithographed board is 11" square and has 8 circles with star in center, 1¾" partition at side holds pieces . **30.00**

Picture Puzzle: Wild Domestic Animals, puzzle, ca 1899, 16½ x 14½", black and white picture of completed puzzle on back of box cover, multicolored and lithographed pieces show all kinds of animals **95.00**

Pillow-Dex, skill, ©1896, 5⁷/₈ x 4", 7+ pieces [several balloons, 2 wooden stoppers, 2 boundary strings weighted by wood blocks, instruction sheet] **20.00**

Ping-Pong, skill, ©1902, 20 x 7½", 13 pieces [2 paddles, 6 celluloid balls, 2 clamp-on bases, 2 stanchions for net, net and instruction sheet], instructions on back of cover, this is first Ping-Pong set Parker manufactured upon purchasing American rights to the game from Hamley Brothers and J. Jaques & Sons, Ltd. of London **150.00**

Pit, card game, ©1919, 5³/₈ x 3¾", 65 cards, advertising card, instruction sheet, cards lithographed, purple, white, and red numbers, backs show large steamship, tug, wharf, etc., game still produced today, original edition produced in 1904 . . . . **10.00**

Pit, card game, 1904, 2¾ x 3½", 64 cards and instruction sheet **10.00**

Polly Put The Kettle On, skill, 1923, $7^5/_8$ x $6^5/_8$", 10 pieces [3 wooden pieces of tripod, black metal kettle, wooden spring for balls, 4 colored wooden balls, advertising card], instructions on back of box cover **30.00**

Pollyanna: The Glad Game, separate board and pieces box, ca 1915, 18¾" square board, matching 6¾ x 3¾" box of 29 pieces [4 dice cups, 8 dice, 16 brass-bound colored disks, advertising card, and instruction booklet], board folds in half **30.00**

Poppin-Ball, skill, ca 1910-12, 8¼" square, instructions on back of cover, multicolored lithographed target board with 16 wooden headed pins protruding from numbers on target and celluloid ball with rattle for throwing at target **25.00**

Popular Game Of Tiddledy Winks, The, Salem Edition, skill, 1897, 26 pieces [4 felts, glass cup, 20 colored bone winks, instruction sheet] **15.00**

Potato Race, skill, 1902, 19½ x 5½", 52 pieces [48 colored wooden "potatoes", 4 tin spoons], directions on back of box cover, bottom of box is sectioned into 4 equal "potato bins" **110.00**

Quit, card game, 1905, 5¼ x $3^7/_8$", 54 pieces [52 cards, advertising card, and instruction sheet], card backs have blue and white water scene **10.00**

Robber Kitten, puzzle, ca 1895-1900, 10½ x 7¾", 2 multicolored lithographed cat puzzles, one is same as cover, other shows cats before fireplace and grandfather clock **50.00**

Rook, card game, Edition D, Rook Card Co., patented March 22, 1910, 5½ x 3¾", 56 cards, instruction booklet, 3 advertising cards, backs of cards have Dutch Canal scene **10.00**

Three Blind Mice,skill, ca 1903, 7¼ x 5¼", 4 pieces [round wooden "mouse trap", multicolored and lithographed on top with woman standing on chair, 3 mice and numbers over each trap opening, and 3 rounded wooden blocks representing mice] instructions on back of box cover **40.00**

Walt Disney's Donald Duck's Party Game For Young Folks, 1938, 19¼ x 9¾ x 1¾" **65.00**

Wide World Game, separate board and pieces box, 1933, $4^1/_8$ x 8¼ x $1^3/_{16}$", 63 pieces [4 metal airplanes, 4 metal ships, 6 passage tickets, 48 travel cards (24 green, 24 pink), gameboard], 4 page instruction sheet, $4^7/_8$ x $6^{11}/_{16}$", track, created by Hendrik Willem Van Loon, illustrations ©1933, Stephen Slesinger, Inc. **75.00**

Yachting, boxed board game, ca 1895, 5¼ x 5¼", 5 pieces [4 round colored wooden counters and wooden die], instructions on back of box covers, multicolored lithographed board with track through water, yachts . . . **15.00**

Yes or No, card game, ca 1910, 7½ x 5½", 13 question cards, numerous printed multicolored answer slips and instruction sheet **10.00**

Young America Target, skill, ca 1895, 9½ x $11^3/_8$", instructions on back of box cover, multicolored lithographed target board is 8¾ x 10¼", with 1" partition for 5 wax balls with different color feathers attached **25.00**

PAUL EDUCATIONAL GAMES

Wyoming, OH   ca 1920's

Heroes Of America, Games Of The
Nations Series, ca 1920's 5½ x 4
x 1" **25.00**

CHARLES M. PEAT

New York, NY   ca 1820's

Geographical Conversation Cards,
card game, 1822, 2³/₈ x 3³/₈", 54
cards [26 hand-painted map cards, 26

question cards, instruction cards, title
card] **150.00**

PHILADELPHIA GAME MFG. CO.

Philadelphia, PA   ca 1910's

Major League Base Ball Game, boxed
board game, 1912, 19 x 13½", 37 pieces
[20 wooden peg players, 6 wooden
score pegs, 2 small red boxes, 9 packets
of line-up cards], bottom partitioned,
12½ x 4½", space contains rules pasted
on bottom, 14 x 4½" space has multi-

colored wheel with 9½" attached
chrome spinner, back of box cover
has multicolored baseball field framed by wooden dovetailed sides (oak),
Honus Wagner, Ty Cobb listed on line-
up cards **800.00**

H. J. PHILLIPS CO. INC.

New York, NY   ca 1920's

Quiz Of The Wiz, The, quiz, ©1921,
5¾ x 3⅛", 130+ quiz cards; picture of Edison on cover signed "J. N.
Ding" **20.00**

PHILLIPS COMPANY

New York, NY

Game of "Keeping Up With The Joneses", The, separate board and pieces box, ©1921, 17½" square board, matching 4¾ x 5¼" box contains 21 pieces [4 dice cups, 2 dice, 16 colored counters, instruction sheet], board folds in half, red, pink, and black track with comic characters in each corner, game play same as *Parcheesi*; A. R. Momand, inventor **85.00**

PIROXLOID PRODUCTS CORP.

New York, NY

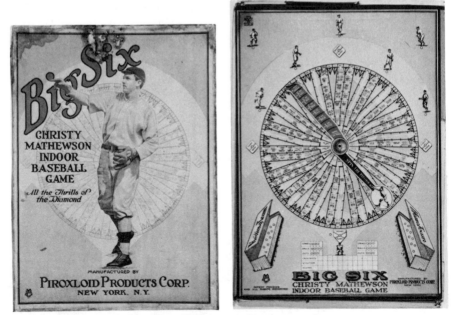

Big Six: Christy Mathewson Indoor Baseball Game, 1922, 16¾ x 22¾ x ¾" **600.00**

PLAY EQUIPMENT CO.

Los Angeles, CA   ca 1930's

Baffel, 1939, 7¼ x 7¼ x ⅝" . . . **20.00**

PLAZA MFG. CO.

New York, NY   ca 1930's

Fiddlestix, skill, ca 1937, 2 x 8½", 111 pieces [110 sticks and instruction sheet], cardboard, multicolored cylinder container **15.00**

THEODORE PRESSER

Philadelphia, PA   ca 1890's

Elementaire, 1896, 4½ x 3½ x ⅞" by M. S. Morris **20.00**

J. PRESSMAN & CO., INC.

New York, NY   ca 1920's

Hop-Over Puzzle, skill, ca 1930's, 6⅝ x 6⅝ x 1½" No. 2991, 9 pieces [game cardboard, 8 marbles (4 black, 4 white], instructions printed on game cardboard, printed 4½ x 2⁹⁄₁₆" solution sheet, frog motif, nine holes in line, multicolored, strategy **20.00**

Flash, skill, ca 1930's 14⅛ x 14¼ x 1⅞", No. 6790 . . . . **25.00**

PRESSMAN TOY CORP.

New York, NY   ca 1930's

Wordy, ©1938, 14 × 14 × 1", similar to Scrabble **25.00**

PUNG CHOW COMPANY, INCORPORATED

New York, NY   ca 1920's

Pung Chow, classic, ©1923, 9¼ x 5¼", 214 pieces [144 tiles, 64 wooden sticks, 2 dice, 2 score cards, 2 instruction booklets], separate black and red 15¼ x 2½" cardboard box holds 4 tile racks **35.00**

RADIO GAMES COMPANY

Peoria, IL   ca 1920's

Game of Radio, card game, ca 1925, 2⅝ x 3⅝", 54 pieces [51 cards, advertising card, instruction booklet], card backs are brown and white, faces show early speakers and radio call letters of different cities **40.00**

RAPAPORT BROS., INC.

Chicago, IL   ca 1940's

Quiz Kids Electric Quizzer, ca 1940, 12¼ x 9⅜ x 2³/₁₆", No. 1000, 5 cards with quiz on each side, cards 10½ x 7½", instructions printed on inside of lid **40.00**

W. S. REED TOY CO.

Leominster, MA   ca 1870's-1920's

The company was first known as "Inventors, Manufacturers, and Exporters of Toys, Novelties and Games." In 1897, the company was absorbed by the Whitney Reed Chair Company, also of Leominster, Massachusetts.

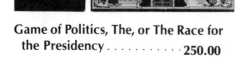

Game of Politics, The, or The Race for the Presidency **250.00**

World Educator and Game, The, 1919, box 14 x 6⅝ x 1¼" **45.00**

REGENSTEINER CORPORATION

Chicago, IL   ca 1920's

Kuti-Kuts (Cutie Cuts): A Comic Cartoon Game, ©1922, $5^5/_8$ x $9^1/_8$ x $^3/_4$" **20.00**

ROOK CARD CO.

(Division of Parker Brothers)

Salem, MA   ca 1910's

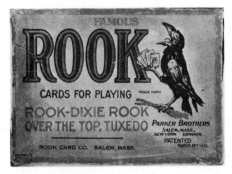

Famous Rook, card game, patented March 22, 1910 . . . . **10.00**

ROSEBUD ART CO.

New York, NY   ca 1920's-30's

Big Apple, ©1938, $11^5/_8$ x $11^5/_8$ x $1^3/_8$", No. 85 . . . . **25.00**

Kitty Kat Cup Ball, ca 1930's, 10 x $14^3/_4$ x 2", No. 80 . . . . **55.00**

Rolawheel (Three In One), 1926, 9¾ x 6⅝ x 1¹³/₁₆", No. 36, board with attached wheel, board has 3 rows of numbers, wheel divided into 12 units, 4-page 2⅝ x 4¾" instruction booklet . . . **20.00**

Soli-Peg, ca 1930's, 10³/₁₆ x 6¼ x ⅞", No. 70 . . . . **20.00**

ROY-TOY COMPANY

New York, NY   ca 1930's

Alee-Oop, skill, ca 1939, 3 x 4½", 22 pieces [21 wooden sticks, 4 wooden bars, instruction sheet], multicolored cardboard cylinder with 'Oscar and His Oops, The Life of The Party" printed on it **15.00**

RUDOLPH TOY & NOVELTY

Play Radio Game **25.00**

RUSSELL MFG. CO.

Leicester, MA   ca 1930's

Comical Game Of Whip, The, card game, ca 1930-32, 6¼ x 4¾", 32 multicolored cards **15.00**

Take-Off, card game, ©1930, 6¼ x 5", No. 529, directions on back of cover, 32 cards, game similar to *Lindy* **20.00**

Game Of Buried Treasure,
The, ... **25.00**

RUSSELL PRESS, INC.

ca 1930's

Game Of Doctor Quack **15.00**

Slap Jack, 1935, No. 54 2⅝ x 3½
x ³/₈" **10.00**

SAALFIELD PUBLISHING CO.

Akron, OH

Animal Game **50.00**

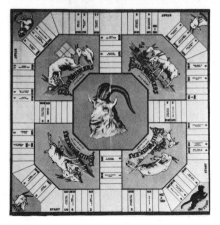

Billy Whiskers, separate board and pieces box, ca 1923-26, board opens to 18¼" square, 6½ x 5¼" pieces box, No. 280, 10 pieces [8 brass-bound counters, spinner, instruction booklet], multicolored lithographed track, board has red and white pictures of ram's head, many goats, Button the Cat, and Billy Whiskers in center **95.00**

Hoot, card game, ca 1926-28, 55 pieces [52 cards, Hooty card, instruction card], cards are multicolored animal characters from the Thornton W. Burgess stories **40.00**

O. SCHOENHUT, INC.

Philadelphia, PA   ca 1930's

Fan-Tel, ©1937, 2½ x 6", 50 pieces [48 flat wooden sticks and 2 instruction sheets] **15.00**
456 Pick Up Sticks, skill, ca 1937, 1⅞ x 8", 42 pieces [41 sticks and instruction sheet], black, orange and white cardboard cylinder **15.00**

E. G. SELCHOW & CO.

PUBLISHERS

New York, NY   ca 1870's

Corn & Beans, quiz, 1875, 5½ x 3½", 42+ pieces [40 cards, 1 question card, instruction sheet and large quantity of corn and beans]; by Albert A. Hill **35.00**
Game Of Witticisms, The, card game, 1878, 5⅜ x 4", 81 pieces [80 cards and instruction booklet], inventor was R. R. Manners **20.00**
Quartette Union War Game, card game, 1874, 2⁹⁄₁₆ x 3⁹⁄₁₆", 49 cards [1 is instruction card], cards are black on white, box has gold letters on purple ground **25.00**

SELCHOW & RIGHTER

New York, NY; Bay Shore, NY   1867-present

Started as a wholesaling operation under Albert B. Swift in 1867, Elisha G. Selchow purchased the company in 1870 and made John Harris Righter a full partner shortly thereafter. They were primarily a jobber until 1927, when they began to make their own games. The company moved to Bay Shore, Long Island, in 1955. Coleco bought the company in 1987, retired the Selchow & Righter name, and then went bankrupt. The company was bought by Hasbro/Bradley, and remaining games are now published under the Milton Bradley logo.

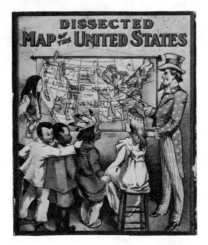

Champs: Land Of Braun, ca 1920's, 15½ x 15½ x 1½" **25.00**

Ed Wynn The Fire Chief, boxed board game, ca 1937, 4¼ x 9", 23 pieces [4 dice cups, 8 dice, 4 colored wooden counters, 4 knobbed sticks, 2 tin pans, instruction sheet] **25.00**

Dissected Map Of The United States, puzzle, ca 1910, 9½ x 11½", multi-colored lithographed **40.00**

Fascination, skill, ca 1890, 6 x 6", 10 pieces [round wooden board, top, 8 red marbles, directions on back of box cover **35.00**

Game Of Old Maid, card game, ca 1890, 4⅝ x 3⅝″, 36 cards and "old maid" cards are same as cards of J. H. Singer **15.00**

Have-U "It?", card game, ©1924, 7¾ x 5¾ x 1″ **20.00**

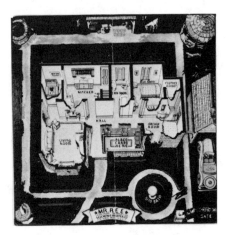

Komical Konversation Kards, ca 1890's, 5⅜ x 4⅜ x 1″ **20.00**

Mr. Ree, separate board and pieces box, ca 1936-38, 18¼″ square board folds in half, box of 119 pieces [4 small metal weapon tokens, 7 character cylinders, 7 character cards, 100 direction cards, instruction sheet], multicolored lithographed board signed by "William Longyear", game played like our modern day *Clue* **50.00**

Sectional Checker Board Puzzle, puzzle, 1880, 5¼" square, 14 red and black checkered pieces **20.00**

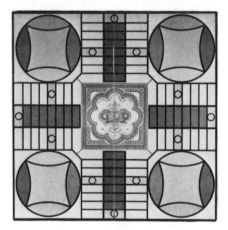

Sliced Nations, puzzle, 1875, 9¼ x 8", 76 straight multicolored cardboard pieces, directions and models printed on box bottom **40.00**

Parcheesi, classic, patented March 17, 1874, folding board opens to 18½" square, 6½ x 3" matching box of 29 pieces [4 dice cups, 8 dice, 16 colored counters, instruction booklet], multi-colored track, with "Home" written in center, trademark was re-registered May 20, 1890 . . . . **20.00**

Pigs in Clover, puzzle, ca 1875, round game 6¼" in diameter, card board maze inside with 5 clay marbles representing pigs, round wooden opening in middle labeled "pen", President Harrison pictured by media playing this game **40.00**

Snake Eyes, card game, ca 1930's, 11 x 7½", No. 27, 185 pieces [120 cards, dice cup, 2 wooden dice, 62 chips], instructions on back of box cover, cards multi-colored with "craps" expressions printed on them. Black theme **55.00**

Vignette Authors **15.00**

War-Whoop,
card game, ©1904, 5¼ x 3⁵/₈″, 52 cards
and instruction sheet **25.00**

Chessindia, boxed board game,
trademark registered March 30, 1915,
8½ x 16½″, 16 pieces [board, 2 dice
cups, box holding 4 dice, 8 brass-
bound counters], directions on back of
box cover, folding board opens to 16″
square, lithographed multicolored, has
fortress in center, and cannon and cannon balls in each corner, *Parcheesi*-
type track **45.00**

Mr. Ree: The Fireside Dectective, 1937,
10½ x 9½ x 1⁵/₈″, No. 77, 121 pieces
[1 gameboard, 4 card board weapons
(hatchet, revolver, knife, and poison),
8 character cards, 8 hollow tokens, 100
playing cards, including 4 murder
cards], 15-page, 3 x 5¼″ instruction
book **35.00**

Snake Eyes, Junior Edition, 1941, 14¹/₈ x
12¾ x 1½″, No. 206, 40 pieces [1 dice
cup, 2 dice, 36 covering cards, 1 game
platform], 5³/₈ x 10″ instruction sheet,
printed both sides **35.00**

THE SHARP CO.

New York, NY   ca 1890's

Sharp's Shooter, bagatelle, ©1895,
10 x 20½″, wood, metal pins and
shooter, black and red lines, instructions and patent information stencil on
back **30.00**

SHULMAN & SONS
(Goody Games)

New York, NY   ca 1930's

Goody Magic Questionnaire, quiz, ca
1932, 13 x 6¾″, 34 pieces [33 question
and answer cards and 1 metal Magic
Reader], instructions on back of snap
leatherette cover, bottom of case divided into 3 4 x 6″ compartments to hold
cards and Magic Reader **25.00**

J. C. SINGER

New York, NY   ca 1890's

Philippines, boxed board game, ca 1898,
10¼ x 12½″, 17 pieces [spinner and 16
wooden counters], game board on box
bottom, lithographed, multicolored,
directions printed in lower right corner,
flags and cannon pictured on other 3
corners, in *Parcheesi*-track format,
game reflects battle of Spanish-
American War **95.00**

J. H. SINGER

New York, NY ca 1883-95

Jasper Singer, known as J. H. Singer, was primarily a jobber of games and novelties, associated with the manufacture of ornate wooden toy theaters. Singer at one time hired George S. Parker to sell his lines. Singer's box covers often just tabeled "J.H.S."

Cuckoo **15.00**

Game Of Authors, card game, ca 1890, 4 x 3", 20 multicolored cards . **10.00**

Game Of Base Ball, boxed board game, ca 1885-90, 5¼" square, 6 pieces [4 round wooden counters, spinner and board which lifts out of bottom], multicolored board shows baseball diamond and players **55.00**

Game Of Jumping Frog, card game, ca 1890, 5 x 4", 21 pieces [20 multicolored cards and instructions sheet], cards represent 10 nursery rhymes in pairs **20.00**

Game Of Letters, card game, ca 1890, 5 x 4" 27 pieces [26 multicolored cardboards with letters of the alphabet and lithographed pictures and instruction sheet] **20.00**

Game Of Old Maid, card game, ca 1890, 4¼ x ¾", 18 cards and "old maid" **15.00**

Mystic Wanderer, The, boxed board game, ca 1890-95, 8¼ x 4¾", 7 pieces [5 multicolored lettered cardboard strips, instruction sheet and footed wooden "planchette" board], planchette, multicolored, lithographed, depicts witch pointing with bats flying about, this game played much like the *Ouija* board **75.00**

Peter Coddles Esq. And His Trip To New York, 4⁵⁄₈ x 5⁷⁄₈ x 1" **20.00**

Steeple Chase, boxed board game, ca 1890, 5¼" square, 8 pieces [6 round wooden counters, spinner, and multicolored lithographed board which lifts out of bottom], board represents track with racehorses pictured in center **15.00**

Telegraph Messenger, boxed board game, ca 1890, 7¼" square, 4 pieces [2 counters, card with spinner and directions, lift out board], board is multicolored cardboard, checkered, with 3 pictures of messenger . **40.00**

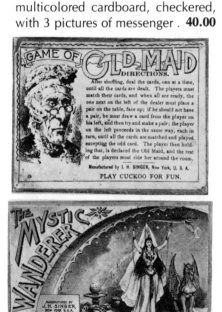

Where Do You Live, card game, ca 1890, $3^7/_8$ x $4^7/_8$", 26 pieces [25 multicolored lithographed cards and instruction sheet] **25.00**

Country Store, The, boxed board game, ca 1890, 12¼ x 7¼", 43 pieces [2 multicolored boards for store set-up, 20 cardboard money cards, 20 merchandise cards] **75.00**

Favorite Steeple Chase, boxed board game, ca 1895, 14 x 9¼", 7 pieces [6 wooden counters and spinner], multicolored lithograph of race track pasted to box bottom, instructions printed in center, pictures show stable, horses, jockeys and dogs **45.00**

Game Of Fox & Geese, card game, ca 1890, 5 x 4", 17 pieces [16 cards and spinner], cards multicolored, show geese, eggs and foxes, directions on cover of box **15.00**

SNOW BROTHERS PUBLISHERS

Worcester, MA   1872

Game Of Snap, card game, 1872, $2^5/_8$ x 4" (no box), 60 cards and instruction sheet **15.00**

SNYDER BROS. GAME CO. INC.

Elmira, NY   ca 1900

Trolley, card game, ©1904, 4¼ x 2¾", 62 pieces [60 cards, instruction sheet, advertising sheet], card faces black and white, backs light brown and white with picture of trolley **45.00**

Trolley, card game, ©1904, 2¾ x $4^3/_5$", 60 cards and instruction booklet, backs of cards are orange and white with picture of trolley car **45.00**

STANDARD TRAILER CO.

Cambridge Springs, PA   ca 1920's

Dad's Puzzler, puzzle, ©1926, by J. W. Hayward, 3¼ x 4", directions on face of cover, 9 plain wooden pieces of different shapes **15.00**

Flying Puzzle, The, puzzle, ca 1926-28, 4¾ x 4", directions printed on face of box, box contains 14 pieces of wood of different shapes, labeled "plane", "clouds", "water", "air", "pocket", etc. **15.00**

Traffic Jam Puzzle, The, puzzle, ca 1927-29, 4¾ x 4", instructions on back of box cover, box contains 14 wooden pieces of different shapes with car labels of "Reo", "Chevrolet", "Garland", "Hudson", "Nash", etc. **15.00**

STAR PAPER BOX CO.

Chicago, IL   ca 1920's

Star Basketball, bagatelle, ca 1926, 19 x 19½", 6 pieces [5 black balls and metal bagatelle board], board multicolored, directions printed in upper left corner, cardboard covered with net "basket" in center, upper right hand corner reads "Starfine Games" **95.00**

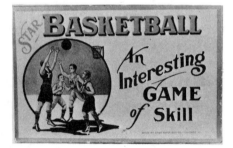

STAR PUBLISHING CO.

ca 1890's

Game Of World's Fair, card game, 1892, 2½ x 3½", 60 cards and instruction booklet, 24 cards from multicolored puzzle of Chicago's World Fair, other cards picture portraits of officers and city officials connected with Fair, 2 different games can be played . . **65.00**

THE STATLER, MANUFACTURING CO., INC.

Baltimore, MD   ca 1930's

United States Geographical Lotto, educational, ca 1930's, 11¾ x 6 x 1", 260 pieces, [20 7³/₈ x 5", map, playing cards, 240 pieces 1½ x ⁵/₁₆" lotto city disks], match the cities with the map segments **20.00**

STOLL & EDWARDS CO., INC.

New York, NY   ca 1920's

Adventures Of Tom Sawyer And Huck Finn, ©1925, 9¼ x 18 x 1½". **120.00**

Fortune Telling Game, card game, ca 1930-32, 2½ x 3¾", 45 cards and 2 instruction cards, backs are blue and white picturing gypsy, faces are red and green with figures **25.00**

Game Of Pegpen, ©1929, 13½ x 13½ x 1³/₈", 2 boxes of playing pegs (first red and yellow, second blue and green), peg board, instructions pasted to inside of lid **30.00**

Game Of Treasure Island, 1923, 8½ x 16³/₈ x 1¼", 21 pieces [spinner, 4 wooden pieces, box of 16 checkers], gameboard 16 x 16", dual game board—checkers on one side, Treasure Island on other **45.00**

STOLL & EISEN GAMES INC.

(Playjoy)

Long Island City, NY   ca 1930's

Dog Sweepstakes, 1935, 10½ x 20 x 1¼" **60.00**

STRAT GAME CO., INC.

New York, NY   ca 1910's

Strat: The Great War Game, ©1915 . . . . **45.00**

PETER G. THOMSON

Cincinnati, OH ca 1880's

Game of Old Maid and Batchelor, card game, ca 1885, 3⅛ x 4⅛", 36 pieces [34 cards, "Old Maid" card and instruction sheet] **25.00**
Geographical Cards, Improved, ©1883, 5¾ x 4¾ x 1½" **15.00**

Anagrams, educational, ca 1885, 6 x 4³/₅", many square yellow lettered cards and instructions card **15.00**
Game of Mythology, The, ©1884, 3¾ x 5⅛ x 1¼" **20.00**

TOY CREATIONS

New York, NY ca 1930's-40's

Official Radio Baseball Game, 1939, 20½ x 13½ x 1½", numerous pieces [cardboard game board, spinner, team roster sheets, team cards, numbered cards, pegs], instructions on back of box lid, game board with baseball diamond and score board, spinner with 25 positions **50.00**
Official Basketball Game, ©1940, 20½ x 13½ x 1½" **40.00**
Official Radio Football Game, ©1939, 20½ x 13½ x 1⅝" **40.00**

TRANSOGRAM CO. INC.

New York, NY   ca 1930's

Big Business, separate board and pieces box, 1937, 9³/₈ x 18³/₈ x 1⁵/₈", game board: 18" square, pieces box: 4⁵/₈ x 6 x 1¼", No. 1211 . . . . **45.00**
Dog Race, 1937, 14⁵/₈ x 10⁵/₈ x 1³/₈", No. 1213 . . . . **35.00**
Lucky Bingo, ©1936, 13¹¹/₁₆ x 7¼ x 1¹/₈", No. 7012 . . . . **15.00**

TRIPS CARDS CO.

Albany, NY   ca 1900-10's

Trips, card game, ca 1905-10, 2⁵/₈ x 3½", 106 cards and instruction card, cards are red and white and black and white, and each shows train and different railroad companies, backs show map of U.S. with railroad routes . . **65.00**

TROJAN GAMES

Minneapolis, MN   ca 1930's

Traffic Hazards, 1939, 21¼ x 13¼ x 1", No. 44 . . . . **45.00**

UNITED GAMES COMPANY

Brooklyn, NY

Frog Who Would A-Wooing Go, The **60.00**
Little Soldier, The, boxed board game, 17½ x 10½", 5 pieces [spinner and 4 wooden counters], instructions on back of box cover, multicolored lithographed track board with black and white picture of soldiers and horses in center, cover has Parker Brothers logo of ship "made in Salem, Mass." in lower left corner **50.00**

THE U. S. PLAYING CARD CO.

ca 1890's-1900

Birds, card game, ©1899, No. 1127, 2¾ x 3¾", 52 cards and instruction card **25.00**
Poems, card game, ©1898, 2¾ x 3¾", No. 1123, 52 cards and instruction booklet **25.00**
U. S. Card Dominoes, card game, 1905, 1½ x 2½", 55 cards and instruction sheet, backs of cards are blue, faces look like dominoes **20.00**
Wild Animals, educational card game, ©1903, 2¾ x 3¾", 55 cards and instruction booklet, lion on card backs **25.00**

UNKNOWN MANUFACTURERS

Autogiro: Pocket Game, 1928, 2½ x 4½ x 1" **20.00**
Catch Raffles, boxed board game, ca 1905-10, 14½ x 8½", 6 pieces [spinner, 4 counters, instruction sheet], board multicolored, lithographed on box bottom has squares with background scenes of "bobbies", Raffles auto, and train, box cover has logo of 2 bees in oval with "New York, Chicago and St. Louis" **75.00**
Chateau Thierry **35.00**

Continents and Products, educational card game, ca 1895, 4⅞ x 3⅞", 5 yellow continent cards and innumerable product cards with instruction sheet **15.00**
Four Puzzled Pigs, The, ca 1880's 6¾ x 6¾ x 1¼" **40.00**

Little Hocus Pocus, card game, ca 1840-50, 8¾ x 4¾" slide wooden box, 81 pieces [32 3 x 3⅞" cards, 12 2⅝ x 1⅞" cards, 36 markers and instruction sheet], cards are multicolored, hand painted, box bottom partitioned into compartments **375.00**

Multiplication Merrily Matched **20.00**

Palmistry, card game, ca 1910, 6 x 5", + pieces [numerous numbered cardboard squares, 4 diagrams of human hand, and instruction and key sheet] **30.00**

Frog Pond, boxed board game, ca 1895-97, 18 x 10", 13 pieces [6 green metal frogs, 6 fishing poles, board], set in board, multicolored lithograph of frogs on lily pads in pond . . . **45.00**

Merry Game Of Old Maid, The, card game, ca 1888, 3¼ x 4¼", 36 cards and "Old Maid", box lithographed on wood **15.00**

Funny Fortunes, boxed board game, un-dated, 10½ x 10¾", 6 pieces [teetotum, 4 counters, folding board], directions on back of box cover, board 10½ x 19¾", multicolored, checker board-type with printed fortunes . . . **45.00**

Game Of Language **10.00**

Grande Auto Race **95.00**

Post Card Game, card game, ca 1905-10, 5¼ x 7¼", 41 cards including instruction card **40.00**

Round Up, The, skill, ca 1900-05, 4¾ x 3¾", 20 pieces [15 checkers, pink tape attached to 5 checkers, 3 cardboard discs, instruction sheet] **15.00**

Rummy, ca 1910, 5³/₈ x 7⁵/₈", 48 cards and instruction sheet **15.00**

Tortoise And The Hare, separate board and pieces box, undated, 5 x 12" wooden board, 3½ x 2¾" cardboard pieces box, 3 pieces [teetotum, cardboard turtle and hare on wooden supports], directions on back of board, board has gray paper track pasted on it **45.00**

Untitled, blocks, Patent No. 597519, 9 x 6", 12 flat multicolored lithographed grooved blocks, and 18 wooden disks with instruction sheet **55.00**

Panama Canal Puzzle, puzzle, 1912, 4 x 1⁵/₈ x ⁵/₈" **75.00**

Panorama Nursery Alphabet, educational ca 1870, 5½" square, multicolored, lithographed, scroll type **325.00**

Veranda **15.00**

Crickets, skill, ca 1890, 4⅝ x 8⅞", 5 pieces [4 brass rings and wooden "wink"], box opens to reveal hearth on back of cover with wooden bowls on mantle and black wooden kettle over fire, bottom of box is multicolored lithographed target, game played like *Tiddledy Winks* **75.00**

Drawing Made Easy, art, ca 1890, 6¾ x 4¾", 12 stencils **15.00**

Game Of Doctor Quack, card game, ca 1922-25, 5⅛ x 6½", 30 cards and instruction sheet **15.00**

Game Of Royalty, card game, ca 1895, 2¾ x 4", 32 cards and instruction booklet **15.00**

Get My Goat, puzzle, 1914, 3¾ x 2⅞", 12 puzzle squares in blue and white, one with head of goat, instructions on back of box cover **10.00**

Happy Family, The, card game, ca 1880, 4¾ x 3¾", 32 cards and instruction sheet, bottom of box carries advertisement for *Pitch-a-Ring* and *Ring Toss* **15.00**

Laughable Game Of What D'ye Buy, The, By Professor Punch, card game, ca 1850, 3 x 4¼", 12 lithographed and hand painted "trades" cards, numerous black and white merchandise cards, and instruction sheet **55.00**

Lotto, classic, ca 1884, 7¾ x 5½", directions on back of box cover, 24 green and white cards, numerous round wooden numbers and box of square glass covers, directions state "Game of Loto" **15.00**

Merry War, skill, ca 1890-1900, 9¾ x 6¼", 9 pieces [3 steel balls, 8 x 5½" spring target plate, 5 blocks of wood with multicolored lithographed soldiers on them, directions on back of cover, target board says "The New Game of Merry War The Childrens Delight. No. 2 Pat. apl'd for." . **40.00**

Play Radio Game, classic, ca 1927, 110+ pieces [10 bingo-type cards, 100 small cards with numbers, numerous cardboard disks for covering spaces], directions on back of box cover . . . **10.00**

Steeple-Chase, boxed board game, trademark  ca 1890-95, 18 x 11½", 16 pieces [6 numbered cards, 6 lead horses on stands, 3 dice, folding board], directions on back of cover, board folds in 4, multicolored, lithographed, pictures race track on both sides, horses, jockeys, grandstand, etc. **95.00**

WARNER MANUFACTURING CO.
Bennington, VT

Major Bowes' Amateur Hour Game **20.00**

SAMUEL WELLER
ca 1840's

Pickwick Cards, The, card game, 1844, 2⅝ x 3¾", 16 cards and title card, cards are deep yellow and green and depict characters from Dickens, created for The Pickwick Club by the inventor, Weller, lithographed by W. S. Francis, New York **150.00**

WESCOTT BROS.

Seneca Falls, NY

Game Of Fish Pond, 12¼ x 3½ x 1³/₈",
No. 12 . . . . **65.00**

WEST & LEE GAME COMPANY

Worcester, MA   ca 1873-76

    The company incorporated in 1874. It manufactured toys and games, and printed rules of various games. The company later became known as Noyes & Snow.

Avilude, or Game of Birds, card game, 1873, 2⁷/₈ x 4", 65 pieces [64 cards and instruction sheet], card faces are black and gray, illustrating different birds **30.00**

Ferrilude or Game of Beasts, card game, 1873, 2⁷/₈ x 4", 65 pieces [64 cards, instruction sheet], card faces are black and white illustrating different animals **30.00**

Totem, card game, 1873, 4½ x 3½", 38 pieces [36 cards, advertising sheet, instructions sheet], cards printed in black and white, with plain backs . . **20.00**

G. M. WHIPPLE & A. A. SMITH

Salem, MA   ca 1860's

Game of Authors, The, card game, 1861, 4½ x 3¼", 80 cards, on back of box bottom is pasted list of games, known as *The Salem Games;* believe this to be the original game as invented by A. A. Smith **50.00**

Squails, skill, 1865, 8 x 4", 18 pieces [metal "procese", 16 round squails, instruction sheet], directions state D. B. Brook & Bro., Boston, as manufacturers, A. A. Smith invented game of Authors in 1861, Glossary of Terms in directions very amusing **75.00**

WHITMAN PUBLISHING CO.

Racine, WI

Charlie McCarthy, Game Of Topper, Edgar Bergen's, ©1938, by McCarthy, Incorporated, 8⅞ x 8⁵⁄₁₆ x 1⅝", No. 2903, 45+ pieces [8 wooden hats, score sheets, 36 cards, stiff paper playing board 8½" square], instructions on back of playing board **45.00**

Charlie McCarthy Question And Answer Game, Edgar Bergen's, card game, ©1938 by McCarthy Incorporated, 8¼ x 5½ x ⅞", No. 3908, 45 cards [22 question cards, 22 answer cards, 1 instruction card], inside of base has cartoon graphics of Charlie and Bergen. **25.00**

Dick Tracy Detective Game, boxed board game, ©1937 by Chester Gould, licensed by Famous Artist Syndicate, 13 x 6½ x 1", No. 3065, 18 pieces [folded cardboard gameboard (12½" square), spinner with 2 circles of numbers, 16 markers, small cardboard squares], instructions on inside of lid, track **80.00**

Dick Tracy Playing Card Game, card game, ©1934 by Chester Gould, 5 x 6½", No. 3071, 36 pieces [1 instruction card and 35 multicolored cards of Dick Tracy, jewels, and gangsters . . **45.00**

Dick Tracy Playing Card Game, ©1937 by Chester Gould, 5 x 6½ x ⅞", No. 3071 . . . . **45.00**

Fortune Telling Game, 1934, 13¹/₈ x 11¼ x 1¼", No. 2096 . . . . **25.00**

Grand Slam, The, card game, ca 1930-32, 54 pieces [52 red and black cards and 2 instruction cards] **15.00**

Hollywood Movie. Bingo, 1937, 9½ x 6⁵/₈ x 1", No. 3046, numerous pieces [spinner (alphabet), 10 cards each with 3 names of movie stars), and 60+ covers disks], cards 6¼ x 4" . **40.00**

Oh Blondie!, 1940, 9¾ x 6 x 1", No. 3019 . . . . **30.00**

Old Hogan's Goat, ©1939, 11½ x 8½ x 1⁵/₁₆", No. 3938, game platform in box, 6 colored marbles, 1 die, instructions printed on inside of box lid . . **20.00**

Pop-Eye: Playing Card Game, card game, ©1934 King Features Syndicate, 6½ x 5¹/₁₆ x ¹⁵/₁₆", No. 3070 . . **40.00**

Game Of Old Maid, card game, ca 1932, 2½ x 3¾", 44 pieces [42 multicolored character cards, 1 "Old Maid", and instruction card], several of the cards are black caricatures **35.00**

Game Of Seven-Up or Help Your Neighbor, The, 14½ x 8½" . . **20.00**

Kentucky Derby Racing Game, 11 x 7" **35.00**

Pick Up Sticks, skill, ©1937, 2 x 8½", No. 2188, 42 pieces [41 sticks and instruction sheet], red, black and white cardboard cylinder **15.00**

WILDER MFG. CO.

St. Louis, MO

ca 1920's

Boards often show "YLDR" symbol.

Combination Board Games, boxed board game, ca 1922, 8¾ x 17", 13 pieces [folding board, 4 metal animal figures, dice cup, 5 dice, score sheets, advertising pamphlet for company], directions for 12 different games on back of box cover, board lithographed, multicolored on both sides and numbered 126 and 128 with patent number **75.00**
Construction Game, boxed board game, ca 1925, 12¼ x 7½", No. 125, 36 pieces [one die, 2 wooden counters, 33 cardboard "supplies"], directions on back of cover, multicolored board pasted on box bottom, logo of company is ◆ **25.00**
Movie-Land Keeno, card game, ©1929, 9 x 7½", 56+ pieces [8 large Keeno cards, 48 calling cards, and large quantity of red markers], directions on back of box cover, calling cards picture famous movie stars of the era, cards are black and white, *Bingo-*type game **95.00**

Ocean To Ocean Flight Game, boxed board game, ca 1927, 7½ x 12¼", 7 pieces [spinner and 6 counters], multicolored lithographed board of U.S. map, directions on board in lower left corner **110.00**

WILKENS THOMPSON CO.

Malden, MA   ca 1900

China, separate board and pieces box, 1905, folding board opens to 18½" square, 2¾" cardboard box of 13 pieces [4 metal horsemen, 8 metal soldiers, and instruction sheet], board multicolored with 4 affixed spinners in each corner, *Parcheesi*-type track . **75.00**

THE WITS COMPANY

Bloomsburg, PA   ca 1920's

Wits, card game, 1922, $2^5/_8$ x $3^5/_8$", 96 cards and instruction sheet with U.S. map, World War I Game **20.00**

F. A. WRIGHT

Cincinnati, OH   ca 1870's-80's

Game Of Moneta, card game, ©1888, 5½ x 4", 51 pieces [50 cards and instruction sheet], game cards represent money coin of U.S. of that era, "By the Author of Logomachy" **25.00**

Logomachy Or War Of Words, card game, 1875, $2^7/_8$ x $3^7/_8$", 56 cards and instruction sheet, blue and white backs of Egyptian figures, game won Silver Medal at Cincinnati Industrial Exposition in 1874 .... **25.00**

W. G. YOUNG & CO.

Chicago, IL   ca 1910's

Spear-Em, skill, 1916, 12 x 6½", 8 pieces [2 wooden spears, 6 cardboard cavalry figures], target game, each horseman representing different country, Willis Young, inventor **25.00**

ZONDERVAN PUBLISHING HOUSE

Grand Rapids, MI   ca 1930's

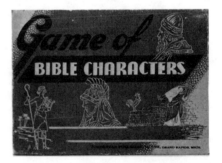

Game Of Bible Characters, ©1939, by Verita V. Blair Head, $7^5/_{16}$ x $5^3/_8$ x 1", 64 pieces [64 cards divided into 16 sets of 4 cards each], 5 x $9^3/_8$" instruction sheet **15.00**

GAME SPECIALTIES

Games sold products. Many companies employed games, usually of the track variety, as a means of conveying their corporate image to the public. Gasoline companies, like the long gone White Rose, dairies, bakeries, sponsors of popular radio programs and many other business organizations used games as premiums to enhance their reputations.

Companies such as Columbia Bicycles also put out "whist" (forerunner of Bridge) counters to help whist players keep track of the points and games. Other concerns used advertising counters in much the same manner as companies dispense advertising pens and calendars to the public today.

Although most of these advertising games and counters were cheaply made and mass produced for giveaways, they make interesting collectibles in the game as well as advertising fields.

Numerous "games" (not games in the true sense) fostered the enjoyment of art. They ran the gamut from coloring and paint sets to stencils, tracing, and mosaics.

Bagatelles comprise a category unto themselves. Although not as large as their modern derivatives, the huge pinball machines, they nevertheless require room to display. Originally, bagatelle games resembled billiards and were played on tables six to ten feet in length, using balls and cue sticks. The cups or depressions for the balls numbered one to nine. The table gradually shrunk in size, and the cue sticks were abandoned for the pull spring mechanism.

Many of the old bagatelles have very colorfully designed boards, which make them very desirable wall hangings. The firm of M. Redgrave of Jersey City, New Jersey, produced the earlier bagatelles, ca 1870-80, and the Lindstrom Tool and Toy Co. of Bridgeport, Connecticut, was a prolific producer of the later ones.

To spend even one dollar for a game a century ago was not always possible for an average American family. Consequently, individuals constructed their own board games. They used whatever was handy—a spare slab of wood, a discarded chair seat or even a cheese box cover. These handmade games often were well executed and brightly painted. Today, collectors consider them a form of folk art, and prices for these have risen dramatically. The most common type, by far, is that of the checkerboard, with *Parcheesi* a close second. Rarer forms represent *Backgammon, Nine Men's Morris, Fox and Geese,* and the *Ouija* board.

Glassed-in lithographed puzzles, often on the back of round pocket mirrors, and the numerous metal ring puzzles, such as those A. C. Gilbert produced, often find their way into game collections. Odd shaped dice, unusual score keepers, postcards with a game motif or even framed prints illustrating game playing make unusual additions to a game collection.

Not to be ignored are two foreign companies who did manufacture blocks and games for the American market. The German company of F. AD Richter was founded in 1508. In the 19th century, they found a representative in the United States and set up a branch factory in Brooklyn, mainly specializing in their well known stone blocks. These architectural sets came in several sizes and are readily found as well as collected today. The company enjoyed a great business in this country until the beginning of World War I forced their take over by this nation's Alien Property Custodian.

J. W. Spear started manufacture well over a century ago in Bavaria and exported many games to this country. The company produced many of the game classics like *Ludo, Lotto,* and *Fish Pond,* and is known for its bright cover lithography on a linen mat-like finish. The years 1886 to the early 1930's saw their most prolific exportation.

Finally, gaming pieces themselves provide unique collectibles. The block spinners, prevalent for only a few years, celluloid, mother of pearl, bone, or ivory counters, wooden and lead figures, clay or glass marbles and hand painted cards all contribute to the overall attractiveness of the game itself.

ADVERTISING

BEECH-NUT PACKING COMPANY
Canajoharie, NY   ca 1910's

Going To Market, card game, ©1915, 2¾ x 3¾", 52 cards and one instruction card, cards have blue and white scene of "Going To Market", all cards show logos and advertisements of products: Beechnut, Libby, Willys-Overland, Welch's, Knox Gelatine, etc., game also marketed by Pompeian Night Cream **110.00**

CHAMPION SPARK PLUGS

Champion Road Race, folding board opens to 18 x 12" multicolored track on cardboard, 2½ x 12" strip on side with cutout spinner and 6 cutout race cars, with printed instructions **40.00**

204

CRISPY TOP BREAD
CUSHMAN BREAD CO.

Crispy Top Bread, 2¾ x 4¼", 48 multi-colored cards collected showed how mail was delivered to 48 countries of the world. **35.00**

Cushman Bread Co., 48 cards collected, educational cards descriptive of American states **35.00**

GIBSON GAME CO.
Boston, MA   ca 1910's

Little Shoppers, ©1915, 28 pieces [4 cardboard shoppers and 24 cardboard products], folding cardboard opens to 20 x 14", multicolored track features ads for Mennen, Ivory Soap, Diamond Salt, and many others **195.00**

E. LEVERING & CO.
Baltimore, MD

Levering's Coffee, folding checkerboard opens to 10" square, yellow and black squares **30.00**

NATIONAL REFINING CO.
Cleveland, OH   ca 1910's

White Rose Gasoline, patented April 29, 1919, 14½" square, multicolored track on paper, reverse side is checkerboard with printed directions, spinner **50.00**

PABST BREWING CO.
Milwaukee, WI   ca 1940's

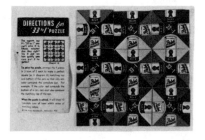

"33 to 1" Puzzle, ©1940, 9 2" square pieces, 2¾ x 5" instruction sheet, printed both sides **25.00**

PHENYO-CAFFEIN CO.
Worcester, MA

Sectional Checkerboard Puzzle, 5¼ x 5¼ x ⅝" **20.00**

PLANTERS PEANUT

Planters Peanut Party, 19¾ x 17½ x ⅝", original version appeared in magazine, ordered large version from company **60.00**

SHELL OIL
ca 1930's

Stop and Go, 1936, 10 x 10¾" multicolored paper track, attached to board is 5½ x 10¾" strip containing 40 cutout gasoline tickets, 4 shell counters, spinner, and instructions, separate red and green sheet has 54 cutout cards **40.00**

STOLL & EDWARDS CO., INC.

New York, NY   ca 1920's

Game Of Ting-a-Ling, The, ©1920, folding board opens to 20½ x 13" multicolored track, spinner attached on lower left corner, 4 counters, directions written on right side, board advertises milk as best food **40.00**

STANDARD OIL COMPANY OF OHIO

ca 1930's

A Bully Time In Spain With Gene and Glenn and Jake and Lona, Sohio Radio jig-saw puzzle No. 3, 1933, 8¼ x 6⅛ x 1¹⁵/₁₆", two sided puzzle **25.00**

WOLVERINE SUPPLY & MFG. CO.

Pittsburgh, PA   ca 1920's

Gee-Wiz Race, mechanical game, 1923, 15¾ x 6", No. 40, instructions on back of box cover, pat. no. 1462189, string attached to wooden ball and metal race track which lifts out, race is operated

by means of fly wheel, track is multi-colored with 6 horses, ball bearing in each track slot **100.00**

Jungle Parts, 21⅝ x 21½" **40.00**

TABLE GAMES

McLOUGHLIN BROTHERS

New York, NY   1828-1920

Game of Six Nations, card game, ca 1865-70, 4¼ x 5¾", mahogany box with slide cover, 42 lithographed cards, hand painted, invented by Elsie Rymer **150.00**

UNKNOWN MANUFACTURERS

Game Of The Fortress, skill, ca 1870, 8" square, all wood peg board, lithographed and hand painted, instructions pasted on back of board, probably had wooden pegs **90.00**

History Of A Plumb Pudding, The, puzzle, 1825, 5¼ x 6½", all wooden puzzle pieces, multicolored lithographed, and hand painted, together with multicolored lithographed, and hand painted series of pictures on paper to use as model for puzzle, wooden box with slide cover, rare, on bottom of box is written "George D. Dodd, a present from his sister Susan D. Dodd 1825" **250.00**

Untitled, bagatelle, ca 1845, 8½ x 16½", all wood with metal pins, wooden pusher for marbles, multicolored lithographed with garden scene at top of board, and numbered slots for marbles at bottom **150.00**

Untitled, bagatelle, ca 1850, 7⅛ x 13¾", 2 wood feet underneath, has wooden spring ball release, multicolored lithographed on all wood, Oriental scene at head of board, numerous pins and ball depressions with 8 number partitions at bottom of board . . . **140.00**

Untitled blocks, ca 1820-40, 5¼ x 3¾", 6 lithographed blocks, making 6 different pictures including one on slide cover, wooden box **150.00**

Untitled, marble game, ca 1880, 4 x 6¼", 14" tall, multicolored lithographed on all wood, clown and small boy pictured on vertical section with funnel at top for marbles, marble hits pins on way down and comes out in one of 3 gold and red alleys marked 3, 10 and 5 . . . . **325.00**

Yellow Kid, board, ca 1890, 3½ x 33¾", multicolored, lithographed . . **395.00**

W. S. REED TOY CO.

Leomister, MA   ca 1870's-1920's

Jolly Marble Game, The, skill, ca 1875, 8¼ x 19¾", height when opened 21", multicolored and lithographed on all wood by Forbes Co., Boston, played with a marble or marbles . . **400.00**

Aces High, bagatelle, Durable Toy & Novelty Corp., New York, ca 1928;-30, 8⅛ x 19 x ⅛", multicolored lithographed metal, 10 balls **85.00**

Auto Race, mechanical, Gotham Pressed Steel Corporation, New York, NY, No. G150, ca 1930, 10⅞ x 21⅞", multi-colored lithographed metal, metal frame, 5 colored metal cars . . **120.00**

Sharp's Shooter, bagatelle, Sharp, New York, NY, 10¼ x 20½", wood, painted red and black heart motif, instructions and maker's label stamped on back **75.00**

GAME MUSEUMS
AND CLUBS

MUSEUMS

Connecticut Valley Historical Museum
Early Milton Bradley Memorabilia
Springfield, Mass. 01101

Museum and Archive of Games
Dr. Elliott Avedon, *Curator*
University of Waterloo
Waterloo, Ontario, Canada N2L 3G1

Washington Dolls' House and Toy Museum
5236 44th Street, N. W.
Washington, D.C. 20015

SLIDE FILM PRESENTATION

Antique American Games
Lee and Rally Dennis
110 Spring Road
Peterborough, N.H. 03458

CLUBS

American Game Collectors Association
4628 Barlow Drive
Bartlesville, Okla. 74006

BIBLIOGRAPHY

Andrews, Peter. "Games People Played," New York, NY: *American Heritage* Vol. 23, No. 4, pp. 64-79, 104-5.

Aries, Philippe. *Centuries of Childhood,* New York, NY: Vintage Books, 1962.

Art Gallery of Nova Scotia. Canadian Gameboards, Nova Scotia: 1981.

Avedon, Elliot and Sutton-Smith, Brian. *The Study of Games,* New York, NY: John Wiley and Sons, 1971.

Banks, Newell Williams. *Scientific Checkers,* Detroit, MI: Morris-Systems Publishing Co., 1923.

Bell, R. C. *The Board Game Book,* Los Angeles, CA: The Knapp Press, 1979.

_____ *Board and Card Games from Many Civilizations,* New York, NY: Revised Edition, Dover Publications, Inc. 1979.

_____ *Board and Table Game Antiques,* Aylesbury, Great Britain: Shire Publications, 1981.

Bradley, Milton, Company. *A Successful Man,* Springfield, MA: 50th Anniversary Booklet, 1910.

Brady, Maxine. *The Monopoly Book,* New York, NY: David McKay Company, 1974.

Carson, Jane. *Colonial Virginians at Play,* University Press of Virginia, 1965.

Culbertson, Judi. "Collecting American Board Games," *The Antique Trader,* Aug. 22, 1984, Vol. 28.

Dennis, Lee. "Do Not Pass Go." *Yankee,* December, 1972, pp. 104-6, 146, 149-50, 152.

_____ "Game Hunting is Big," *Spinning Wheel,* September, 1967, pp. 10-11, 40.

_____ "Games Americans Played," *Historic Preservation,* January-March 1977, pp. 28-31.

_____ "Games People Played," *Yankee,* February, 1978, pp. 158-173.

_____ "Games People Played," *Collectibles Illustrated,* Vol. 1, No. 1, May/June 1982, pp. 46-49, 80, 83.

_____ "Games People Played," *Time/Life Encyclopedia of Collectibles,* Vol. 7, 1978, pp. 46-59.

_____ "It's All in the Game," *Cobblestone,* July, 1980, pp. 19-22.

_____ "Old American Games," *Hobbies,* August, 1971, pp. 48-9, 62.

Diagram Group. *The Way to Play,* New York, NY: Bantam Books, 1977.

Frazer, Antonia. *A History of Toys,* New York, NY: Hamlyn Publishing Group. 1972.

Freeman, Dr. Larry. *Yesterday's Games,* Watkins Glen, NY: Century House, 1970.

Freeman, Ruth and Larry. *Cavalcade of Toys,* Watkins Glen, NY: Century House, 1942.

Garis, Roger, *My Father Was Uncle Wiggily,* New York, NY: McGraw Hill, 1966.

Goren, Charles H. *Goren's Hoyle Encyclopedia of Games,* New York, NY: Chancellor Hall, Ltd., 1961.

Grunfeld, Frederic V. *Games of the World,* New York, NY: Holt, Rinehart and Winston, 1975.

Hency, Robert. "Board Games," *Rarities*, Vol. 3, No. 4, July/August 1982, pp. 36-39, 64-65.

Hewitt, Karen. *Toys As a Cultural Resource*, Montpelier, VT: Department of Libraries, 1980.

Hewitt, Karen and Roomet, Louise. *Educational Toys in America: 1800 to the Present*, Burlington, VT: University of Vermont, 1979.

Hoffman, Marilyn. "Antique Games," *Christian Science Monitor*, May 18, 1984, pp. 21.

King, Constance E. *Antique Toys and Dolls*, New York, NY: Rizzoli International Publications, 1979.

_____ *Encyclopedia of Toys*, New York, NY: Crown Publishers, 1978.

Love, Brian. *Play the Game*, Los Angeles, CA: Reed Books, 1979.

_____ *Great Board Games*, New York, NY: Macmillan Publishing Co., 1979.

McClintock, Inez and Marshall, *Toys in America*, Washington, D.C. Public Affairs Press, 1961.

McClinton, Katharine Morrison. *Antiques of American Childhood*, New York, NY: Clarkson N. Potter, Inc., 1970.

Mebane, John. *The Coming Collecting Boom*, New York, NY: A. S. Barnes and Co., Inc., 1970.

Murray, H. J. R. *History of Board Games Other than Chess*, London: Oxford University Press, 1952.

Parker Brothers, Inc. "75 Years of Fun," Salem, MA: 1958.

_____ "90 Years of Fun," Salem, MA: 1973.

_____ "100 Years of Fun," Salem, MA: 1983.

Provenzo, Asterie Baker and Eugene F., Jr. *Play It Again*, Englewood Cliffs, NJ: Prentice Hall, 1981.

Pullar, Elizabeth. "Games Children Played a Century Ago," *Spinning Wheel*, September/October 1982, pp. 16-19.

Scheller, William. "Massachusetts Companies Make Famous Games," *MassBay Antiques*, December, 1983, pp. 1,8,17.

Schroeder, Joseph, Jr. *The Wonderful World of Toys, Games & Dolls*, Northfield, IL: Digest Books, Inc. 1961.

Selchow and Righter. "The First Century of the Selchow and Righter Company, 1867-1967."

Shea, James Jr., as told to Mercer, Charles. *It's All in the Game*, New York, NY: G. P. Putnam, 1960.

Shea, James, Jr. "The Milton Bradley Story," Princeton, NJ: University Press, 1973.

Speare, Elizabeth George. "Child Life in New England," Sturbridge Village, MA, 1972.

Wood, Clement and Goddard, Gloria. *The Complete Book of Games*, Garden City, NY: Country Life Press, 1940.

INDEX

213

OTHER TOPICS COVERED BY WALLACE-HOMESTEAD

All of the following books can be purchased from your local bookstore, antiques dealer, or can be borrowed from your public library. Books can also be purchased directly from **Chilton Book Company, One Chilton Way, Radnor, PA 19089-0230.** Include code number, title, and price when ordering. Add applicable sales tax and **$2.50** postage and handling for the first book plus 50¢ for each additional book shipped to the same address. VISA/Mastercard orders call **1-800-695-1214** and ask for Customer Service Department (AK, HI, & PA residents call **215-964-4000** and ask for Customer Service Department). Prices and availability are subject to change without notice. Please call for a current Wallace-Homestead catalog.

COLLECTOR'S GUIDE SERIES

Code	Title/Author	Price
W5339	Collector's Guide to Baseball Cards, *Troy Kirk*	$12.95
W5479	Collector's Guide to Early Photographs, *O. Henry Mace*	$16.95
W5320	Collector's Guide to American Toy Trains, *Susan & Al Bagdade*	$16.95
W5568	Collector's Guide to Autographs, *George Sanders, Helen Sanders, and Ralph Roberts*	$16.95
W5487	Collector's Guide to Comic Books, *John Hegenberger*	$12.95
W5649	Collector's Guide to Treasures from the Silver Screen, *John Hegenberger*	$16.95
W5347	Collector's Guide to Quilts, *Suzy McLennan Anderson*	$17.95
W572X	Collector's Guide to Toys, Games & Puzzles, *Harry L. Rinker*	$14.95
W5762	Collector's Guide to Victoriana, *O. Henry Mace*	$17.95

COLLECTIBLES

Code	Title/Author	Price
W5258	American Clocks and Clockmakers, *Robert W. & Harriett Swedberg*	$16.95
W5703	The Authorized Guide to Dick Tracy Collectibles, *William Crouch & Laurence Doucet*	$12.95
W4529	British Royal Commemoratives with Prices, *Audrey Zeder*	$24.95
W4464	Check the Oil: Gas Station Collectibles with Prices, *Scott Anderson*	$18.95
W4723	Clock Guide Identification with Prices, *Robert W. Miller*	$14.95
W5541	Collectible Kitchen Appliances, Price Guide to, *Gary Miller and K. M. "Scotty" Mitchell*	$17.95
W6041	Collectible Pin-Back Buttons 1896–1986, *Ted Hake and Russ King*	$19.95
W5916	Coca-Cola Collectibles, Wallace-Homestead Price Guide to, *Deborah Goldstein Hill*	$15.95
W569X	Collecting Antique Marbles, Second Edition, *Paul Baumann*	$17.95
W5460	Commercial Aviation Collectibles: An Illustrated Price Guide, *Richard Wallin*	$15.95
W4731	Dolls, Wallace-Homestead Price Guide to, *Robert W. Miller*	$16.95
W4936	Dr. Records' Original 78 RPM Pocket Price Guide, *Peter A. Soderbergh Ph.D.*	$12.95
W5681	Drugstore Tins and Their Prices, *Al Bergevin*	$17.95
W5118	Food and Drink Containers and Their Prices, *Al Bergevin*	$16.95

W4901	Girl Scout Collector's Guide: 75 Years of Uniforms, Insignia, Publications & Keepsakes, *Mary Degenhardt and Judy Kirsch*	$21.95
W5797	Greenberg's American Toy Trains, From 1900 with Current Values!, *Dallas J. Mallerich III*	$17.95
W5185	Guide to Old Radios: Pointers, Pictures, and Prices, *David & Betty Johnson*	$16.95
W5711	Hake's Guide to TV Collectibles, *Ted Hake*	$14.95
W5436	Herron's Price Guide to Dolls, *R. Lane Herron*	$16.95
W3060*	Illustrated Radio Premium Catalog and Price Guide, *Tom Tumbusch*	$34.95
W5371	Jigsaw Puzzles: An Illustrated History and Price Guide, *Anne D. Williams*	$24.95
W121X*	Oil Lamps: The Kerosene Era in North America, *Catherine M. V. Thuro*	$38.95
W5312*	Petretti's Coca-Cola Collectibles Price Guide, *Allan Petretti*	$29.95
W4944	Plastic Collectibles, Wallace-Homestead Price Guide to, *Lyndi Stewart McNulty*	$17.95
W5169	Presidential and Campaign Memorabilia with Prices, Second Edition, *Stan Gores*	$18.95
W541X	Psychedelic Collectibles of the 1960s and 1970s: An Illustrated Price Guide, *Susanne White*	$21.95
W5657	Space Adventure Collectibles, *T. N. Tumbusch*	$19.95
W4154	Steiff Teddy Bears, Dolls, and Toys with Prices, *Shirley Conway & Jean Wilson*	$17.95
W538X	Steiff Toys Revisited, *Jean Wilson*	$18.95
W5789	Stereo Views: An Illustrated Price Guide, *John Waldsmith*	$22.95
W4847*	Thimble Collector's Encyclopedia: New International Edition, *John von Hoelle*	$35.95
W1236	Thimble Treasury, *Myrtle Lundquist*	$12.95
W3972	Tins 'N' Bins, *Robert W. & Harriett Swedberg*	$16.95
W4642	Tobacco Tins and Their Prices, *Al Bergevin*	$16.95
W5584	Tomart's Illustrated Disneyana Catalog and Price Guide, Condensed Edition, *Tom Tumbusch*	$19.95
W6033	Tomart's Price Guide to Golden Book Collectibles, *Rebecca Greason*	$21.95
W4140*	Zalkin's Handbook of Thimbles & Sewing Implements, *Estelle Zalkin*	$24.95
W4383	Yesterday's Toys with Today's Prices, *Fred and Marilyn Fintel*	$14.95

COUNTRY

Code	Title/Author	Price
W4499	Antiques From the Country Kitchen, *Frances Thompson*	$16.95
W5428	Baskets, Wallace-Homestead Price Guide to, Second Edition, *Frances Johnson*	$16.95
W5002	Country Sourcebook, Second Edition, *Elaine Hawley*	$19.95
W3263	Graniteware Collector's Guide with Prices, *Vernagene Vogelzang & Evelyn Welch*	$16.95
W4588	Granite Ware, Book II, *Vernagene Vogelzang & Evelyn Welch*	$18.95
W3581	Kitchens and Gadgets: 1920 to 1950, *Jane Celehar*	$16.95
W4251	Kitchens and Kitchenware: 1900 to 1950, *Jane Celehar*	$15.95
W443X	Shaker: A Collector's Source Book II, *Don & Carol Raycraft*	$15.95

FURNITURE

Code	Title/Author	Price
W4758	American Oak Furniture, Revised Edition, *Robert W. & Harriett Swedberg*	$16.95
W5878	American Oak Furniture, Volume II, Second Edition, *Robert W. & Harriett Swedberg*	$16.95
W5886	American Oak Furniture, Volume III, Second Edtion, *Robert W. & Harriett Swedberg*	$16.95
W4111	Country Furniture and Accessories with Prices, *Robert W. & Harriett Swedberg*	$16.95

W376X	Country Furniture and Accessories with Prices, Book II, *Robert W. & Harriett Swedberg*	$16.95
W3883	Country Pine Furniture, Revised Edition, *Robert W. & Harriett Swedberg*	$14.95
W5401*	Macdonald Guide to Buying Antique Furniture, *Rachael Feild*	$25.00
W393X	Victorian Furniture, Book I, Revised, *Robert W. & Harriett Swedberg*	$16.95
W5207	Wicker Furniture: Styles and Prices, Revised, *Robert W. & Harriett Swedberg*	$14.95

GENERAL

Code	Title/Author	Price
W4189	Antique Radios: Restoration and Price Guide, *Betty & David Johnson*	$14.95
W5274	Antiquing in England: A Guide to Antique Centres, *Robert W. & Harriett Swedberg*	$16.95
W5614*	Bessie Pease Gutmann: Her Life and Works, *Victor J. W. Christie*	$29.95
W5304	Buy Art Smart, *Alan S. Bamberger*	$12.95
W5126	The Complete Collector's Guide to Fakes and Forgeries, *Colin Haynes*	$15.95
W5592	Flea Market Handbook: How to Make Money Selling in Flea Markets, Co-ops, and Antiques Malls, Second Edition, *Robert G. Miner*	$12.95
W3913	Flea Market Price Guide, Fifth Edition, *Robert G. Miller*	$12.95
W4121	Jewelers' Circular-Keystone Sterling Flatware Pattern Index, Second Edition, *Binder*	$69.95
W4618	Joy of Collecting, *Harry Rinker & Frank Hill*	$ 6.95
W4855	Oriental Antiques & Art: An Identification and Value Guide, *Sandra Andacht*	$19.95
W5266	Rinker on Collectibles, *Harry L. Rinker*	$14.95

GENERAL PRICE GUIDES

Code	Title/Author	Price
W5509	American Country Antiques, Wallace-Homestead Price Guide to, 10th Edition, *Don & Carol Raycraft*	$14.95
W3921	Antiques, Wallace-Homestead Price Guide to, 11th Edition, *Dan D'Imperio*	$14.95
W5576	Warman's Americana & Collectibles, 4th Edition, *Edited by Harry L. Rinker*	$14.95
W5924	Warman's Antiques and Their Prices, 25th Edition, *Edited by Harry L. Rinker*	$13.95

GLASS

Code	Title/Author	Price
W4308*	American Cut and Engraved Glass of the Brilliant Period, *Martha Louise Swan*	$35.00
W5177	Contemporary Fast-Food and Drinking Glass Collectibles, *Mark E. Chase & Michael Kelly*	$16.95
W5452*	Early American Pattern Glass—1850 to 1910: Major Collectible Table Settings with Prices, *Bill Jenks & Jerry Luna*	$29.95
W4626	Glass Signatures, Trademarks, and Trade Names, *Anne Geffken Pullin*	$16.95
W4421	Pattern Glass, Wallace-Homestead Price Guide to, Eleventh Edition, *Robert W. Miller & Dori Miles*	$15.95
W5444*	Perfume and Scent Bottle Collecting with Prices, Second Edition, *Jean Sloan*	$35.00
W5754	Tomart's Price Guide to Character & Promotional Glasses, *Carol and Gene Markowski*	$21.95

JEWELRY

Code	Title/Author	Price
W3697	Antique Jewelry with Prices, *Doris J. Snell*	$14.95
W5746	Collectible Costume Jewelry, Revised Edition, *S. Sylvia Henzel*	$16.95
W5231*	Ladies' Compacts of the 19th and 20th Centuries, *Roselyn Gerson*	$34.95

PAPER EPHEMERA

Code	Title/Author	Price
W460X	A Collector's Guide to Autographs with Prices, *Bob Bennett*	$14.95
W4987	Currier & Ives: An Illustrated Value Guide, *Craig McClain*	$16.95
W5363	Hancer's Price Guide to Paperback Books, Third Edition, *Kevin Hancer*	$16.95
W5029	Military Postcards, 1870 to 1945, *Jack H. Smith*	$19.95
W5193*	Postcard Companion: The Collector's Reference, *Jack H. Smith*	$39.95
W5673	The Price Guide to Autographs, Second Edition, *George Sanders, Helen Sanders, & Ralph Roberts*	$21.95

POTTERY & PORCELAIN

Code	Title/Author	Price
80038*	British Studio Ceramics in the 20th Century, *Paul Rice and Christopher Gowing*	$45.00
7982X	A History of World Pottery, Revised and Updated Edition, *Emmanuel Cooper*	$27.95
W5398*	Macdonald Guide to Buying Antique Pottery & Porcelain, *Rachael Feild*	$25.00
W0116	Warman's English & Continental Pottery & Porcelain, *Susan & Al Bagdade*	$18.95

* Denotes hardcover, all others are paperback.